MW01068553

SWIPE
TO THE
ALTAR

YOUR 10-STEP ROADMAP TO
FINDING TRUE LOVE ONLINE

MRS. Q. WARNOCK

© 2020 Mrs. Q. Warnock (Qianlei Li)

All rights reserved. This book or any portion thereof may not be reproduced or used in any manner whatsoever without the express written permission of the publisher except for the use of brief quotations in a book review.

ISBN 978-0-578-68208-2

For my Bread Dough,
who made all of my dreams come true,
with love.

YOUR 10-STEP ROADMAP TO FINDING TRUE LOVE ONLINE

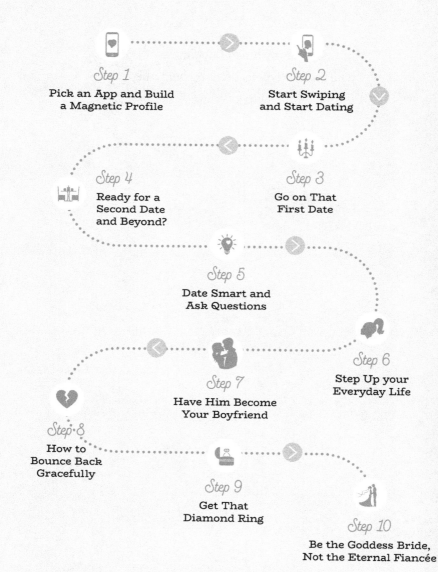

Step 1
Pick an App and Build a Magnetic Profile

Step 2
Start Swiping and Start Dating

Step 4
Ready for a Second Date and Beyond?

Step 3
Go on That First Date

Step 5
Date Smart and Ask Questions

Step 7
Have Him Become Your Boyfriend

Step 6
Step Up your Everyday Life

Step 8
How to Bounce Back Gracefully

Step 9
Get That Diamond Ring

Step 10
Be the Goddess Bride, Not the Eternal Fiancée

Contents

Step 7

HAVE HIM BECOME YOUR BOYFRIEND 137

Step 8

HOW TO BOUNCE BACK GRACEFULLY 159

Step 9

GET THAT DIAMOND RING 167

Step 10

BE THE GODDESS BRIDE, NOT THE ETERNAL FIANCÉE 187

Introduction

Where did all the single, straight, and emotionally available guys go? In 2019, 45 percent of the US population, or around 148 million people, were single. We don't know exactly what the percentage is for single and emotionally available men, but it isn't zero. Why does it seem unfeasible to have one of them as your boyfriend?

Dating seems to be Mission Impossible for women nowadays. Online dating is supposed to make it easier, but in reality, you either don't meet up after chatting all week or it turns out later that he isn't interested in anything more than one night. Dating experts have written countless books and made numerous videos on the topic, but either the advice is too hard to apply in real life, or it's not specific enough and not broad enough to cover all aspects of online dating.

The good news is that this book can take you by the hand and teach you how to walk every single step in online dating;

from downloading the correct app to having him eager to be your boyfriend when you are ready. You will learn how to create a magnetic online profile and spot the right guy to go out with. You will discover the foolproof way to get him hooked past the third date, and I promise you it's not what you have in mind. You will develop the powerful mindset to boost your confidence and become the person who is absolutely irresistible to the right guys. You will also know what to say word for word in undesirable circumstances. When you are ready for marriage, this book will reveal the unspoken truth of how to get the proposal you always wanted, and how to really become the bride, rather than stuck as an eternal fiancée.

I had always been the most single girl I knew and never thought I would get married one day to an amazing guy. Guys I liked were either gay, had girlfriends, or they were not interested in me. The few guys that did approach me to ask me out were either unattractive to me, boring, or players. I went to a speed dating event in summer of 2014 and encountered more awkward and weird men than ever before. They just weren't what I was looking for. I ended up talking to other female participants about how terrible the event was and turned it into a career informational interview in the end. I was slowly losing hope and started to give up finding love... At the end of 2014, my friend introduced me to online dating, so I decided to give it a try.

I went on more dates than I can remember. After seeing enough players, casual daters, and people that were nothing like what they claimed to be, eventually I met this guy that I thought was finally going somewhere. He ended up breaking my heart. Now that I look back, he was full of red flags screaming at me, trying to show me that he wasn't remotely the guy I thought he was. I simply couldn't or wouldn't see those red flags.

After 41 first dates, I finally met the guy that later became my husband. I am so glad he was the 42nd, because if he showed up before I found the correct way to go about online dating, I would have missed him. I went on those 42 first dates during more than two years' time and learned the keys to online dating the hard way.

I learned all of these lessons and wrote this book so you don't have to learn the hard way. If you want to get married one day, but find it nearly impossible to find a boyfriend in real life, this book is for you. If you have thought about trying online dating but don't know where to start, this book is for you. If you are back in the dating field after a divorce or have already tried online dating, but aren't getting the desired results you deserve, this book is for you. This book is the last one you need to read before you say, "I guess online dating just isn't for me."

I am going to tell you the brutal truth. Does your online profile need an update? Are you not attracting high-quality matches? I can help you navigate the world of online dating, translate the language of communicating with someone online, and help you realize your worth. There are a lot of pitfalls in trying to get to know a person online or long distance. This book will help you recognize mixed signals, understand the best methods for meeting in person, and give you the tools to approach online dating with confidence and boldness.

If online dating is completely new to you, I assure you that if you follow each step and approach it exactly the way I have outlined, you will be going out with guys that you find attractive. If you have already tried online dating and they seemed to only be interested in texting you, I promise that they will ask you out if you follow my methods. If you stopped using online dating because you always end up with the guy that is emotionally unavailable, I assure you that you will find it substantially easier to spot "players."

However, if you are completely reluctant to meet with strangers at all, this book is not for you. If you are curious what online dating is about but you're not looking for anything serious here, this book isn't for you. If you are not resilient enough to be OK with encountering failure and moving forward, this book isn't for you. If you are not a go-getter and hope you can do nothing and your future husband will find you, this book isn't for you. If you expect online dating to be easy and aren't willing to put in the extra effort to follow my guidelines, this book isn't for you.

In fact, *don't* read this book unless you are interested in having an amazing boyfriend and ultimately getting married to the love of your life. Following the steps and using the text message suggestions in the book will make guys fall for you, so please only use them if you are ready to start a serious relationship.

Don't be the girl that dreams about meeting the love of her life but doesn't do anything about it. Be the girl that grabs this book now, downloads the right app tonight, and goes on the first date by this Friday. Be the girl that has friends who tell you "Your boyfriend is so sweet! I can't believe you met him online." Be the girl that walks down the aisle toward the love of her life in front of family and friends.

Are you ready to start now and find your new love as soon as possible, or are you going to let uncertainty and fear hold you back? Are you going to show up to holiday parties with your new boyfriend by the end of the year, or are you going to regret not taking action earlier? Are you going to be happily married in five years to someone you meet online after reading this book, or are you going to lie on the bed, waking up in the middle of the night, wishing you did something different years from now? I know you will make the right choice.

Overview

MYTHS ABOUT ONLINE DATING

"Online dating be like: We've found your match:
99% Compatibility. Location: Pluto."

—UNKNOWN

Who Is Online Dating For?

Y ou've probably seen her. She is one of those women who always look fabulous and are effortlessly surrounded by good quality guys. They barely remain single for long, if at all. Are you one of them?

I'm not. I always felt shy around guys, especially handsome ones. If I saw anyone in my everyday life that I would love to go on a date with, it was always a fierce battle in my mind to get the nerve to go up and talk to him. These brief encounters usually ended the moment his girlfriend came back from the bathroom or he left before I had the courage to go up to him. Even when I finally got the balls to approach and talk to a guy, I got all nervous. Before I knew it, I was once again awkwardly mumbling nonsense so cringeworthy that if I thought about it later, I would want to dig a hole and bury my head in it. My only option of dating was with guys that approached me first, and most of the time, I wasn't attracted to them. When I started a new job and really got to meet many new guys, nothing happened between us more than saying "Hi" to each other in the hallway.

All of my friends either had a boyfriend or were taking a break from dating. I was always the most single person. I just wanted to date someone I liked! Of course, I wanted a boyfriend and eventually a husband, but I couldn't even date attractive guys. In my daily life, I didn't know if guys were into me or if they were even looking for a relationship at all. I spent so many nights googling "where to meet single guys." I went to happy hours and meetup groups. Wherever I went, I always found myself surrounded by girls. I made a lot of girlfriends but wasn't going anywhere in terms of dating. I was only 23 years old and my parents were already setting me up with guys! I was stuck in a harsh and embarrassing dilemma: I wasn't attracted to most guys that approached me or asked me out, while guys that I found attractive were either gay, had girlfriends, or they were never approachable. I tried all the pick-up lines and nothing worked.

If you were nodding along while reading and can relate to my experiences, online dating is for you. It's so much easier to meet new guys online that are available and attractive. Not all of them are really single, like they claim to be, but online dating opens up a bigger selection of potential boyfriends that are only a swipe away. Also, in the world of online dating, most guys approach girls first once they are matched. Responding to a potential suitor's message online is much easier than approaching them face-to-face in real life.

Isn't Online Dating Only for Hookups?

Maybe online dating wasn't the right place to look for something serious twenty years ago. However, an increasing number of people are looking for love online. According to a 2016 study done by Pew Research, "41 percent of Americans know someone who uses online dating and 29 percent know someone who has met a spouse or long-term partner via online dating."[1] It is especially true if you live in a big city. Admittedly, a good number of online daters look for nothing more than a night, but it is up to you to screen them out. With my techniques, you can avoid dealing with people looking only for hookups.

Is There a Stigma with Online Dating?

Who cares? If that's a concern, you can stay away from one of the best tools in the current dating world because of other people's opinions and remain single as a result. Or, you get over it and find your true love online. Your goal is to increase your chances of finding love, and online dating is a powerful tool to make it happen faster. If you really want a relationship, you are going to find it. All the couples I know that met through online dating are proud that it is different from the old boring "we met in a bar" or "we went to college together." Have some fun with the fact that you are adventurous and that you are unique!

---

1   https://www.pewresearch.org/internet/2016/02/11/15-percent-of-american-adults-have-used-online-dating-sites-or-mobile-dating-apps/

Is Online Dating Safe?

The world of online dating is just a small part of the whole world that we live in. There are safe aspects and shady alleys that can be dangerous to the untrained. Watch out for yourself, use my guidelines, and keep in mind that scammers take advantage of people online, just like in other places in our real life. Be smart and you will be fine.

What Is the Magic Number?

How many first dates do you need to go on before meeting the love of your life? Really, finding "the one" doesn't mean there is only one person that can eventually be your husband. Although you will only have one husband, that doesn't mean only one person has the potential to be marriage material. You are looking for someone that you love and loves you, someone that meets your requirements as your future husband, and someone that is in the phase of his life where he is ready for a committed relationship that ultimately leads to marriage. Far more than one person can be "the one," and online dating is going to substantially accelerate the process of meeting your potential future husband.

It took me 42 first dates to meet my husband. I wanted to quit after I went on three first dates because I thought that third guy "broke my heart." Now that I think about it, he was just a normal guy loaded with obvious red flags and I was attaching too much emotional investment to first dates. Unfortunately, I simply couldn't read the warning signs. I wanted to quit again after I went on seven first dates. This time because all the guys I ended up matching with were not really attractive to me and I couldn't get any good-looking guy to swipe right on me. After changing my picture and self-introduction on dating platforms with my friends' help, I started getting matched with guys I was attracted to and really began to enjoy the process. However, happy days didn't last long.

I met the ninth person, we hit it off, and he actually did break my heart tremendously. It took me a month to start going on dates again, and it took me a year to get over him. I stopped doing everything I enjoyed and spent as much time as possible trying to meet guys and go on dates. All I wanted was to find someone like him. The next six first dates I went on were all disappointing. It seemed impossible to meet any guy who was decent both online and in real life. I wanted someone who was attractive both physically and personality-wise, and who also wanted a real relationship. Was that too much to ask?

During that time, I went to Philadelphia with my friend and stayed in an Airbnb. The host couple were in their 40s and they met online. I blurted out, "No way! You are so lucky! I've already gone on enough dates and it's not going anywhere. Clearly online dating isn't for me." Only then did she tell me that he was her 45th first date. After learning that I had only been on ten or so first dates, she told me to keep going. To this day, I am super thankful for her because I knew I would definitely have given up without hearing her story.

I decided to keep going. I made a deal with myself to go on 45 first dates before stopping. I knew I wanted a boyfriend. In fact, I wanted to get married one day. I knew I deserved it. However, things went contrary to my wishes and my dating situation got worse and worse. One day I realized that my life was miserable, and I was depressed. I asked myself: *If it took me ten years to find a boyfriend, would I be willing to spend ten years of my life being miserable?*

That moment was a game changer. I started prioritizing my happiness over the anxiety to find a boyfriend ASAP. I started doing things that I put off when I was too busy going on dates. I picked up my hobbies and focused on self-improvement. I spent at least an hour working out every day, six days a week. I picked up Erhu, also called Chinese Violin, which was the instrument I grew up playing. This even led to me being invited to perform on various occasions. I also continued making videos for my YouTube channel.

Instead of spending so much time on dating apps, I only swiped and responded to messages and texts with the fragmented time I had. When I went on first dates, I focused on just staying positive and having a good time, instead of constantly wondering whether this person could be a possible boyfriend. Interestingly enough, more guys than ever were suddenly waiting to go out with me, partly because of how interesting I sounded, how full my personal life was, and how hard it was to secure a date with me. I was finally getting the hang of how online dating should be done! Almost magically, I was also meeting more high-quality guys in real life who asked me out after a casual conversation, which had never happened before.

Eventually I met my husband on the 42nd first date. So, was 42 the magic number? Not really. It wasn't the number that made a difference. It was because I had transformed into the charming version of myself that was happily busy with my single life and knew how to interact with guys the right way from the beginning. He happened to have appeared at the perfect time. There is no fixed number of first dates guaranteed to meet someone special. The number is going to be different for everyone and it is meaningless to give yourself a limit or wait for a certain number to hit. You should pay attention to every single detail in the roadmap I'm about to unveil and follow every single step. Forget the number.

Recap

- ✓ Online dating is for you if it's hard for you to find guys to date from real life.
- ✓ 29 percent of Americans know someone who has met a spouse or long-term partner via online dating.
- ✓ Online dating doesn't need to be stigmatized. It is a powerful tool to expand your chances of finding love faster.
- ✓ Online dating is a part of our world that has both safe and dangerous aspects.
- ✓ The magic number is different for everyone and it is meaningless waiting for the number to hit.

Step 1

PICK AN APP AND BUILD A MAGNETIC PROFILE

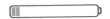

"Anything worth having doesn't come easy."

—GARY HOPKINS

This step is probably the most important one in the entire book. To maximize your success in online dating, promise yourself that you won't skip any steps. Each step builds upon the previous content, so it isn't wise to use this book as a dictionary. This chapter will show you what your principles and priorities should be, which dating app you should use, help you build a magnetic profile, and learn key points of online dating.

Before You Download the App

"Begin with the end in mind" is the second habit of Stephen Covey's book *The 7 Habits of Highly Effective People*. It means to have an end goal in mind, and that everything you do now needs to align with that goal. Having a goal is super important on your online dating journey. If you are reading this book, your goal is probably to find your future husband and get married. Remember this goal, think about why you started online dating, and remind yourself along the way that you are dating with the purpose of finding a great potential husband and eventually getting married.

The journey of finding your future husband online may be new and exciting now, but it will get confusing and frustrating somewhere down the road. Nothing in life that is worth having comes easily. Therefore, it is important to remind yourself of your end goal every day. No matter how attracted you might be to certain guys you meet during the journey, you must delete them from your life if they don't contribute to this end goal. This is your principle.

You Are Your Top Priority

No matter if this process is going to take you only one first date or 45 first dates, you should make *yourself* your top priority the entire time. Your health, your career, your hobbies, your family, and your friends should all be your top priorities. It doesn't matter how hot your new date is; he needs to put in the effort to climb his way up your priority list and meet your requirements. You shouldn't set aside your goals and requirements to justify dating someone who doesn't meet your standards.

Making yourself a priority in life involves two layers. The first layer is rather intuitive. For example, if you have plans with your friends this Friday night, and a new Mr. Hot asks you out last-minute Friday evening, you need to prioritize your friends and stick to your original plan. If you need to stay home one weekend and study for the certificate training crucial to your job, being asked out by that new Mr. Hot shouldn't affect your plan to stay at home and study.

The deepest layer of putting yourself first is to realize your worth. This is the ultimate weapon that will make you irresistibly attractive to guys, and it will be the lifesaver to prevent you from potential heartbreak when things go south.

The core of realizing your value and embracing your confidence is that deep down, you know you are enough, and you know you deserve the great love you've always wanted. When someone doesn't like you or doesn't appreciate you the way you deserve to be, it is *his* problem. No matter if he looks like John Heder or Zac Efron; it is *his* problem. He does not deserve you and needs to be deleted from your life.

I want you to tell yourself "I'm enough" as the last thing before you go to bed, and the first thing when you wake up. Change that to your phone password and write it on your mirror. You are enough, and you deserve a great guy to be your amazing husband one day. Until then, YOU are always your top priority.

Feeling Desperate VS. Acting Desperately

When I was actively looking for a boyfriend, I heard a lot of dating experts say: "Don't act desperately." Desperation, which often comes off as being needy or clingy, is probably the number one thing that kills a new romance. Acting desperately means to be willing to do anything for a man so he will be in a relationship with you. It is the opposite of being high value. Acting desperately can also refer to the woman who suddenly agrees with all of a guy's opinions and loves all of his hobbies.

Feeling desperate means having the urge to find true love. It is that frustration and longing inside you that prompts you to put in the effort to be the best version of yourself and take advantage of opportunities to meet new guys.

It is completely normal to feel desperate. We all want and need love to live the best life that we deserve. It can definitely feel somewhat anxious and nerve wracking if we are not having much luck in finding love. However, you should avoid desperate behaviors. Acting desperately, for example, giving a man your time, attention, and affection (or more), before he has earned anything from you, or pushing down your own feelings and interests to cater to a guy's hobbies or desires, will only bring hurt and sadness. It will also make him perceive you as too eager and a little needy.

When you feel anxious and have the impulse to engage in desperate actions, remind yourself that this behavior is only going to attract guys who want a girl they can take advantage of and push you further away from finding true love. Instead, follow along with the steps in this book and you will be able to make better decisions, be your best self, and find your dream love.

The word "desperate" as it is used in this book is just shorthand for those types of behaviors that could lead to hurt and disappointment. You want to avoid those actions so that you won't be seen as a person with low standards. If you see yourself in some of the negative examples, please don't be offended as I am only referring to the behaviors. After all, you are reading this book so you can be seen and respected as the high value woman that you truly are.

The Best Dating App

If you are looking for your future boyfriend and ultimate husband, does it mean the best dating app should target people looking for a serious relationship? The answer is no. Websites like Eharmony and Match.com are designed for people looking for a serious relationship. However, in my experience, guys on these platforms (especially those using the paid service) can come off a bit too desperate. All they seem to care about is whether you are wife material and how long it will take to get married. To make it worse, some of them won't make an effort to impress you because they think you will automatically date them in order to get married sooner. Some of them assume you are also a bit desperate and undervalue you.

If those websites are not the best online dating platforms, what is the best dating app? The answer is simple: There is no best dating app. Dating apps are like restaurants. You may love it and recommend it to your friends, but some of them may hate it. Your experience with dating apps will vary from mine.

Although there is no best dating app, there is one dating app that you must use. The app that is most popular among guys: Tinder. Tinder is the first app guys think about when they think about online dating. It is where almost every single guy is, and certainly where you should be. I know Tinder used to have a reputation for hookups only, but that is definitely not the case anymore. I personally met my husband on Tinder after my friend met her boyfriend there, and I know of many couples who met on Tinder. After all, there are guys just looking for hookups on any dating app, including the ones that advertise looking for a serious relationship and true love.

You don't need to avoid a certain app (especially the most popular dating app) just to avoid a single type of bad guy. I will show you how to write your self-introduction and communicate online in the right way that conveys your intention. At the end of the day, it is up to you to narrow down which guys you are going out with. You are in control.

Also, I encourage you to try different dating apps and use two or three at the same time in addition to Tinder. Having your profile on more than one app is only going to increase your chance of meeting more guys. However, if you find yourself overwhelmed or burned out, I would keep at least one other app along with Tinder.

Another app that is increasingly popular among guys is Bumble. This app requires women to send out the first message within 24 hours of matching. Personally, I am not a big fan of that. I think guys should make the first move online, considering how relatively easy it is compared to going up to ask women out in real life. Also, the match will disappear unless he responds to you within 24 hours. Thinking about perfect words to message guys in that limited timeframe is extra pressure that you probably don't need in your life. However, if you find this appealing and would like to be in charge of who is able to talk to you, Bumble is a good choice.

Hinge is another newish dating app that is popular among younger guys in their 20s to 30s. Before 2018, Hinge was based on your friend circle on Facebook, so it sounds legit and relationship focused. But, it is a great example to illustrate the discrepancy between the app developer's target user and the real users. In my experience, most guys I matched with on Hinge were only looking for something physical or they were not consistent enough in communication, so we never made it to the first date. Nevertheless, I know women that met their boyfriends on Hinge.

Coffee Meets Bagel is yet another app where some people have had success in finding love. The downside is that it only sends you a few profiles every 24 hours, so it could take three to four days just to spot one guy that you would like to go out with. Ideally, you should have at least two first dates per week, so it is far from enough. However, if you prefer only receiving very limited matches a day, or if you are on a semi-break from online dating, Coffee Meets Bagel is perfect for you.

Happn is a dating app that matches you with people you have crossed paths with. It monitors where you are. Once another user has been to a location you've recently passed by, he shows up on your matching feed. It gives you something to talk about either on the app or on the first date, but Happn is still not very popular among singles, even after being on the market for four years. This app won't appeal to some people who don't want their location monitored.

OkCupid is the first dating app I tried. The excellent part is that it asks you pages of questions before matching you with anyone, so it has a sophisticated matching algorithm. The problem is that it requires you to write paragraphs of answers when building your online profile. Many guys think it's too much work to do for online dating. Potential good guys may not use the app and it is in your best interest to not miss the chance of meeting them.

Apart from these free apps, there are some dating apps that are exclusive and require payment. Let's take The League as an example. Not only do you need to pay, you also have to be approved based on income and Instagram followers in order to join. I don't recommend using it as your only dating app, because having a connection with someone may not depend on their Instagram followers or income. In addition, not all high-quality guys are willing to pay in order to be considered. However, if you are happy to pay for a prescreened group of guys and would like to use it along with other dating apps, go for it.

There are also several dating apps that are based on religious beliefs and lifestyle, such as Christian Mingle, JDate, Asian Dating, and Farmers Only. Definitely look into these options if it is a priority that your future husband needs to share the same religion or lifestyle as you. Otherwise, it may not be a good idea to put yourself out there on these apps.

At this stage, your goal is to meet as many single guys as possible by using dating apps. On every app, there are going to be different kinds of users looking for different things from you. App developers attempt to target a certain group of people, but at the end of the day, it is impossible to really screen guys based on choosing which app you use. Anyone can use any app and it's up to you to use your best judgment as you screen the guys yourself.

Build A Magnetic Profile

Basic Info

What should you put on your profile? Let's take Tinder as an example. Except for the basic info including name, age, and sexual orientation, be sure to put your education, career, and city. Highlighting your education will make you appear more attractive to guys and your career will give them an easier time to start a conversation with you. It is also important to include your city, as most apps use it as part of their main algorithm.

Self-introduction

Every dating app requires you to write something about yourself. Some apps call it "About me" or "Bio." One of the most commonly asked questions is: What should I put in my self-introduction? Apart from the pictures, this is the most important part of your profile.

The easiest way to stand out from the crowd is to *not* leave it blank. You will notice that many people don't even have a bio. If you are browsing Tinder and you see a fairly good-looking guy with no bio, are you more or less likely to swipe right (approve/like) on him? If he couldn't be bothered to take five minutes and write about himself, he probably isn't worth your time or energy. The same rule applies for you, too. Writing something on your bio sets you apart from a good number of girls out there.

There are a million ways to write an attractive bio depending on what you want to get from the platform. The goal is not to write the cleverest or funniest bio on the dating app. Your objective is to have a bio that can represent who you truly are while being appealing to high-quality guys. It also needs to correspond with your attractive and engaging pictures to get more matches. Simply put, your bio should be a short and sweet summary of yourself with a positive and inviting tone, showing your high value and standards.

Let's look at some typical bios and break down what works and what can be improved.

First, take a look at Christina's bio:

> *"I am originally from Buford, Wyoming. It is a small town and I grew up with a brother and two sisters. I moved to Connecticut for college and have been working as a bank tailor. I have been in the area for almost four years since I graduated. Because I work very hard, it's not easy for me to meet new people. After a day's work, I like getting Five Guys to go and watching Netflix on my couch. If I get adventurous, I may go to Buffalo Wild Wings and watch sports there."*

Be honest with me. When did you lose your interest and stop reading it? This bio was more of Christina's boring life story than a cute summary. Your bio should be short: three to four sentences, maximum five. Also, please make sure everything is spelled correctly. I'm sure Christina meant to write "bank teller." She also may want to specify that Five Guys is a restaurant to avoid sounding scandalous.

Next, let's take a look at Ariel's bio:

> *"Half-Japanese, half-German. Moved here three years ago. Don't even bother to message me if you are not six feet tall, don't have six-pack abs, or make less than six figures a year. Bonus points if you have a fabulous fashion sense."*

This bio is short, and it does convey standards, but it is cold and distant; nothing sweet or classy, let alone positive and inviting. If you come up with such a condescending bio, I doubt you would bother to get to know him.

How about Sandra's bio?

> *"I'm pretty shy because I'm new to the city, but I don't bite. I'm looking for a guy to be my boyfriend. Common pick-up lines work most of the time and people always say I am a nice girl! Please message me!"*

This one is short and sweet, relatively positive and definitely inviting, but it screams desperate and low value. Your bio should be attractive and inviting to encourage guys to get to know you, not send out a desperate vibe that is almost begging him to swipe right on you. Also, please avoid including "I'm looking for a guy to be my boyfriend," as it seems too eager at this point.

Again, your bio should be a short and sweet summary of you, have a positive and inviting tone, and show your high value and standards. Here is a formula for you to refer to when you are writing yours:

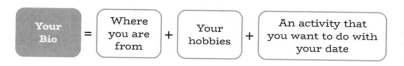

Now that we have the formula down, here comes the second rule: Instead of using abstract adjectives to describe yourself, give specific examples. Rather than just saying you are sporty, say your favorite day starts with an outdoor run. Instead of saying you are artsy, say you love spending time in an art gallery. Mention the most random or last-minute trip you've taken as opposed to just saying you are spontaneous. You get the idea.

When it comes to your hobbies, you want to include ones that show your talents and passions. For example, if you are learning a second language, training for a 10k run, or are passionate about food and are looking for a good restaurant, write about it! However, if you like eating potato chips on a couch while watching Netflix on your low days, don't lead with that. If you like shopping your whole weekend away, it's probably better to let him know about this later.

If you follow all the points mentioned so far, you should already have a good bio. Now it's time to take it to another level. We all have more than one hobby, and it is especially attractive if your hobbies seem to be in sharp contrast with each other. In other words, the more unrelated the two hobbies you list are, the more appealing you will seem. For example, someone who likes watching sports is not likely to be expected to enjoy playing the violin. Someone who is crazy about doing maintenance on their own car is not likely to be a fashionista. A person who likes backpacking excursions may not be expected to show up in a cute little dress. Take a minute to think about the hobbies you have and try to list two hobbies that are vastly different from each other. This takes your bio to an irresistible level.

Let's apply these three principles and see how they transform the bios we saw before.

New bio for Christina:

> *"Sports fan from Wyoming, excited to meet new friends! Enjoy playing the violin and also love watching ESPN after a busy day at work. Let's grab a drink together and see whose team wins!"*

Ariel's new bio:

> *"Japanese-German Grease Monkey. I enjoy getting under the hood of my car and doing my own maintenance. Also love fashion! Let's get some schnitzel and discuss the latest Coyote engine!"*

Sandra's improved bio:

> *"Sunshine Florida girl new to New York City, excited to meet new friends! Love spontaneous backpack excursions and going to Broadway shows in a cute little dress! Let's get outside and have a fun conversation!"*

Pictures

Your pictures need to be attractive and showcase that you are well-rounded. Most platforms allow up to six pictures, and I recommend at least five pictures. Here is the breakdown: You want to have one head shot with a big beautiful smile, one full body picture, one showing off some skin, one with you doing something fun, and one group picture. The pictures should match what you write in your bio.

The headshot with your big beautiful smile should be your main cover picture. Who doesn't like seeing a big smile? Girls with a smile appear more approachable to guys. If you are self-conscious about your smile or think you don't have a perfect supermodel smile, don't worry. A big and confident smile that conveys your positive and joyful inner self is all that you need to capture his attention. If, however, you are one of the girls that have a gorgeous toned or curvy body, or you are more confident with your full body shot, use that one as your cover picture instead.

When it comes to showing off some skin, the key word here is "some." If you want to show off your legs in your favorite miniskirt, keep your top covered. If you want to draw attention to your gorgeous collarbones in that V-neck shirt, keep your legs covered. If you look fabulous in that fitted top with a pencil skirt, keep your cleavage covered. The idea is to show off your sexy side without coming across as slutty. Your main photo can also be a photo of you in an athletic top and a pair of running shorts or in a one-piece swimsuit on a paddle board if you are looking for a sporty, outdoorsy guy.

The next picture should capture you doing something fun, like playing an exotic music instrument, smiling at the camera with your puppy, or holding the Swiss flag on the Alps. You get the idea. Last picture is a group picture. We are usually more comfortable and relaxed taking pictures with our friends, especially if you are camera shy. A group picture of you and your friends happily hanging out also conveys the message that you like having fun and you have your own fulfilled life outside of the dating scene.

Also, remember to make sure your pictures convey the same values as your bio: sweet and classy and showing different aspects of your attractive personality. To be specific, If you say you like running, put a picture of you running in tight sports attire that shows off your curves, or a picture of you stretching after the run. If you say your dog is your best friend, make sure to snap a clear and cute picture with Fido smiling at the camera with you. If you say that you are a mad scientist, make sure to have a picture of you in your lab coat. Your pictures and your bio should give the same idea about who you are.

Recap

- Remind yourself that you are dating with the purpose of finding a great husband and eventually getting married.
- You should always be your top priority, not some hot guy.
- Although there is no best dating app, there is a dating app you must use: Tinder. It is the most popular dating app among guys.
- Your self-introduction should be a short and sweet summary of you, have a positive and inviting tone, and show your high value and standards.
- Your pictures need to be attractive, showcase your personality, convey your well-rounded life, and match your self-introduction.

Step 2

START SWIPING AND START DATING

"One guy said he 'used to be in a band.'
I was like 'That's not an occupation.'"

—JULIE KLAUSNER

eep in mind that you are not just swiping to pass time. You are swiping to find your next boyfriend! Here is the rule: Only swipe right if you are attracted and if you are happy to go on a date with him. Some people recommend you should swipe right on any guy and date as much as possible as practice. The idea is that no matter if you are attracted or not, swiping right on as many guys as possible will eventually allow you to be at your best dating performance when you meet the perfect match. That may work in an ideal world. However, in the real world where you and I live, it can cause you to burn out early and it makes online dating not as fun. Swipe with this question in mind: Would I be willing to go on a date with him?

Look, I said swipe right only if you are attracted. I didn't say only when you are *super* attracted. Let's face it, most straight guys don't necessarily know what picture they look the best in. In fact, straight men are simpler than women when it comes to appearance. They may not even know what shirt looks best on them. So, don't be too picky when you are swiping. However, if you see their pictures contain items that you strictly see as a dealbreaker, then save your future self some trouble and swipe left (reject). If you don't want to be married to a smoker, then don't swipe right if you see a hottie smoking in his backyard. If you are attracted to their pictures, even just a little, go ahead and read their profiles.

When you read his self-introduction, pay attention to what you see and how you feel upon reading. To be specific, read carefully what he wrote, and check if it aligns with the qualities of a man that you want your future husband to have. If you see a conflict, please do yourself a favor by swiping left immediately. Don't expect him to change. I'll say it again. Don't expect him to change. If his last name is "Smith" and his profile says "I'm looking for Mrs. Under Smith," You know he is looking for nothing more than sex. Don't expect him to fall for you, suddenly become a family man, and want a Mrs. Smith.

If his profile screams out negativity and you don't want to spend your life tiptoeing around him and constantly being the sunshine to brighten his world, you know you shouldn't swipe right. Don't expect him to become more cheerful after dating you for a while. If it is important for you to have a husband that has a good relationship with his family, be alert when you read something like "I'm usually barhopping unless I'm trapped in family crap." Don't expect him to change into a family-oriented guy just because it's what you want.

In-App Messaging

Now that you both have swiped right, it's time to message each other in the app. Normally, guys reach out first. If their message includes what you put in your profile, that's a good sign. If your profile mentioned that you are a YouTuber, he might ask "What kind of videos do you make on YouTube?" That means he has read your profile carefully and is interested in having a real conversation with you. In this case, respond to him positively and sweetly, giving him praise for spending time reading what you wrote.

If their message is a question that you obviously have mentioned in your profile, that's usually a sign that they are not looking for anything serious. In this case, don't give him more attention than a short response. For example, if your profile says you are from Shanghai and their first message was "So, where are you from?" feel free to call them out and respond with "You'd know it if you've read my profile," and move on with your life.

I have Three Rules of In-App Messaging (and an overall "Bonus Rule"). You want to highlight this part or bookmark this page, since I will be referring back to this section throughout the book.

1. Keep it short and sweet.

    In-app messaging is not a real conversation. It is also not texting. The only purpose of in-app messaging is to have just enough chats to reach a point where he feels comfortable asking for your number or asking you out. You want to keep your messages short and save long conversations for when you actually meet in person. Also, keep your messages positive. If the message you send out doesn't read positivity or fun, send something else. I'm not telling you to lie. We all have ups and downs. You may not feel the best when you see his message pop up, but your goal is to keep him interested, move things forward, and meet him in person so he can get to know the real you. For this to happen, your message needs to be positive and fun.

2. Match the intensity of his message.

If he doesn't say "You look beautiful in that dress," don't respond with "I love your eyes." If he doesn't ask you how your weekend is going, don't ask him about his weekend. If he doesn't ask you out for a drink or coffee, don't be the one asking him out. However, if he opens up by paying you a compliment, and you are really interested in him, pay the compliment back. I'm going to give you some examples to copy and paste, but feel free to edit them to your liking. If he asked you "What did you do this weekend?" feel free to ask him "Do you have any fun plans this coming week?" If he playfully texted "Looks like you are a pizza connoisseur," be bold and respond with "I see you are a good judge of fine bourbon." You get the idea.

3. Only respond to his message at your convenience.

I'll repeat: Only respond to his message at your convenience. I don't care how attracted you are to his profile. You are always your top priority. You will see this sentence multiple times throughout the book, and it is especially true at this stage when he hasn't made any effort in pursuing you yet. In fact, I recommend you don't even check your dating apps unless you have a moment.

This also makes it easier for the messages you send to appear more composed and interesting. Lots of guys send "How is your day going?" as the first message. If you check the apps multiple times when you are bored, chances are that you will type "It's going. How about yours?" However, if you wait until you have finished your workout and have a free moment, you probably will send something like "Just got out of the gym, it was a great workout." This kind of response is fuller and gives a better image of yourself.

4. Bonus Rule: Be mysterious.

    What if you need to do something else in the middle of the chat? Keep your mystery while excusing yourself. Simply say "I have to go, talk to you later!" In this early stage, you don't even know him yet, so of course he doesn't have the right to know what you are up to. If he doesn't ask you, don't say "I have to get ready for tomorrow, goodnight," or "I need to go help my roommate with something, can we talk later?" Remember, he hasn't earned that much from you yet.

What if he keeps messaging you for more than two days and still doesn't mention meeting up? Gradually lower his priority in the group of guys that you message on the apps. To be specific, don't message him until you are done messaging with all other guys. Increase the time you take to respond. If he still doesn't take the hint, feel free to call him out. Send a message like "Hey I've had fun messaging you, but I'd prefer doing this in person. I'm not one of those girls who are here to message my time away." Remember, you have a life, and you are looking for a guy that at least has the balls to ask you out. If he cannot step up his game and move this messaging relationship to an in-person date, he is out.

How should you respond if you are interested in him, but he only messaged you "Hey"? In my experience, I've never gone out on an actual date with anyone who sends "Hey" as an opener. "Hey" shows that they refuse to put in any effort in talking to you. Chances are that they are sending this generic "Hey" out to a bunch of girls at the same time! They probably have not even read your profile. If they have done so and still cannot come up with anything better to say, are you sure you are interested in talking to them?

If you are really attracted and want to give him one more chance, tease him a bit. Say something like "Do you wanna pretend you said something more fun than that and start over?" or "That is for horses." If you are not a teasing type of girl, or if this guy is one of the most attractive matches you have got, say something like "I normally don't respond to that, but you seem to deserve another chance."

What if he doesn't message you after the app alerts you with: "You've got a match"? There could be millions of reasons, and the easiest path is just to ignore it and move on. If you still haven't received anything from him after a couple hours, you can message him first, but don't put any more attention or thought into it after the message is sent.

Some apps, like Bumble, require women to initiate the conversation within 24 hours of the match. In this case, shoot him a short and sweet message. Ask a question about one of his hobbies mentioned on his profile. If he likes hiking, ask him where his favorite place to hike is. If there is an interesting picture that he posted, ask him about it. Just be short and lighthearted about your message. If you have to be the one reaching out first, like on Bumble, don't send the message right away after being matched. If you swipe right during a bored moment at work and the app immediately alerts you that you have a match, message him after you are done with work. If you swipe right at the end of the night, message him the next day when you have a moment. Don't come off as desperate and remember that you have an amazing life.

Four Types of Guys You'll Encounter

In my experience, there are four types of guys that are on dating apps. There are guys that look for a girl to keep an texting relationship in order to feed his ego, the guys who are only up for casual dating, the type that is ready for something serious if it works out, and the men that are only looking for sex partners.

The texting relationship guys would text you over and over diligently for days, or even weeks, but won't ask you out. The men that thrive on having casual fun with women are those that probably check most of the boxes when you are on a date, but won't move the dating relationship forward. They are either looking for a rebound or they are not ready for a serious relationship. The sex-hunting folks are usually straightforward about it. Some ask you right from the beginning, while others come off as good dating material for the first couple conversations but all of a sudden, they say something that throws them out of the game. For example:

Austin: So you wanna hang out sometime?

Me: What do you have in mind?

Austin: Jamming out is fun. You play an instrument?

Me: Yup I play Erhu, Chinese Violin.

Austin: Cool. Into casual sex?

In this situation, you could simply ignore him. If he is super attractive and you'd like to give him another chance, do this:

Austin: Cool. Into casual sex?

Me: Nope I'm not into casual hookups.

Austin: Darn I would love to meet you.

Me: We are not gonna work.

Austin: You are hot though.

Me: Thanks, you seem fun too.

Austin: How many dates until sex?

Me: It doesn't matter, we are not gonna meet up.

Austin: Lol harsh! Hypothetically, how long until sex?

Now it is time to ignore him because you know the only thing he is looking for is sex.

One way that can help you figure out which type of guy your new match is and whether he deserves a first date with you is by asking this question: "What are you looking for here?" If you are feeling adventurous and you feel attracted enough to go on a date with him already, go ahead and throw the question out casually on the first date. If he asks you back, say something like "Going on dates and see where things go. If the person turns out to be special enough, it could turn to something real, but I don't do casual hookups." You don't have to take this answer word for word, but your answer should convey the fact that you are looking for a serious relationship in an attractive and meaningful way.

Major Traps

If you are new to online dating or you are dating after divorce or a long period of being single, you definitely need to be aware of traps and scammers. There are two major traps. On Tinder, there is a trap called a Tinder Bot, which is an artificial account. Tinder Bots usually have attractive guys' pictures as profiles, but there is no real person behind it. It is only a computer program. The first message they send you tends to appear normal, but the following messages are either one or two words long or gibberish. Eventually, they ask you to "Click on that link." For example, if you text "Can you believe it rained so heavily last night?" He goes "Good! Click on this link!"

The link either leads to a virus or a website that scams money from you. I know it could be discouraging if this happens to you not long after you start using Tinder. However, don't let this be the reason that stops you from using it. After all, it is the most popular app among single guys and it doesn't happen to a lot of Tinder users. In fact, I didn't even know about the Tinder Bot when I was using it. It's fairly easy to spot a Bot. Even if the profile is a hot guy, you are wasting your time flirting with a computer program and may invite a virus onto your device. Keep in mind that a lot of dating apps and social media platforms have their own version of a Tinder Bot.

The second major trap is called Catfishing. Catfishing, different from Tinder Bot, does have a real person behind the profile. However, it isn't the same person as the profile claims to be. For example, the profile picture could be as handsome as Robert Pattinson, but the real person behind the scenes may be a woman who looks like a walrus. It doesn't even have to be the same gender!

The main reason that a Catfisher talks to you is to gradually build up an emotional relationship with you and probably start asking you for money once they have won your trust.

Most of the time, they do this to multiple people at once. They sweetly text you throughout the day and call you to kiss goodnight before you go to bed. They promise to meet up as soon as they can, but they are just too busy travelling for work at this moment. They make you feel that they are already your sweet and charming boyfriend, even if you haven't met them yet.

You keep thinking you are going to meet up soon, but really, you have no idea when that will happen. All of a sudden, they either go through bankruptcy, cannot pay their rent, or they are travelling overseas and their bank account is frozen. They ask you to send them money so they can fly back to see you. Some Catfishers just like to cause chaos or get an ego boost from tricking people into falling in love with them.

Here is a trick to spot Catfishing: A Catfisher will not meet up with you in person. They come up with all kinds of excuses to not meet up. They also often claim to have broken phones and can't FaceTime or video chat. This is also another reason why you must meet your matches in person as early as possible. If they refuse to meet up, you refuse to keep talking to them. You are on this dating app to find a real husband that you can spend the rest of your life with, not a virtual "boyfriend" that lives in your phone.

Take It Offline ASAP

After you've started talking with your new match on the app, take it offline ASAP. It saves you time and cuts off scam daters that take advantage of good-hearted and naive women online. Follow the three rules when messaging in the apps: Keep your messages short and sweet, match his intensity, and only respond at your convenience. If he is serious about getting to know you, he will meet you.

In my experience, most guys ask for your phone number before they set up a meeting plan. Give him your number only if you are comfortable with it. If you are not, message him something like "I will probably give you my number after we meet in person (smiley face)." If he asks for your number without mentioning meeting up in person at all, be sure to convey your expectations. Say something like "Are you asking so you can ask me out later (winking face)?" If he responds by letting you know he is not looking for anything beyond a texting partner, time to tell this attention seeker that he needs to look elsewhere. "Having a pen pal is awesome, but I'm on here to actually meet people."

If you have exchanged numbers, wait for him to text you first. If you two have already planned to meet up before exchanging numbers, it is normal if he doesn't text you afterward.

It may seem at first like a red flag that he is a player or he isn't that interested in you. In reality, you are still strangers and it is understandable to save the conversation for the first date. Actually, back when my husband asked me out on a date when we were talking on Tinder, he asked for my number, but didn't text me at all. He didn't think it was necessary to text me, because we already had a date set up. If you want, you can message or text him one day before the set date and ask "Hey! Are we still on for tomorrow?"

Is it a red flag if he asks for your number or asks you out only after a couple conversations? Not necessarily. Some guys are more comfortable taking their time to approach you before feeling confident enough to ask you out, while others do it as soon as possible to save time, in case you are not interested in meeting up. After all, there are many girls on dating apps that are not looking for a real in-person dating relationship. In fact, when my husband and I matched on Tinder, we only exchanged messages for three rounds before he asked me out. This is what it looked like:

Him: When you say YouTuber, do you mean
             you make videos?

Me: Yeah I make videos and post them on my channel
             when I have time, very procrastinating tho lol.

Him: Haha. What are your videos about?

Me: Good Chinese restaurants in the DMV area!

Him: So would you be willing to meet up in DC
             tomorrow night?

Me:	I've already got plans tomorrow night. How about Friday night?
Him:	Sound good! If you like whiskey we could meet at Jack Rose at 7:30 then go from there.
Me:	I'm not a big drinker and I usually do beer if I drink.
Him:	How about CoCo Sala for some hot chocolate then?
Me:	Sounds more like it! I'm down!
Him:	:D Ok I'll see you then. Btw my number is XXX-XXX-XXXX, the app sometimes doesn't work.
Me:	Cool. XXX-XXX-XXXX.

Recap

- Swipe with this question in mind: Would I be willing to go on a date with him?

- Keep the in-app messages short and sweet, match his intensity, only respond to his message at your convenience, and stay mysterious.

- Four types of guys you will encounter: texters, casual daters, relationship-ready material, and sex-seeking folks. Ask your match: "What are you looking for here?"

- Major traps: Tinder Bots and Catfishing.

- After you've started talking with your new match on the app, take it offline ASAP.

Step 3

GO ON THAT
FIRST DATE

*"If we meet offline and you look nothing like your
pics, you're buying me drinks until you do."*

— UNKNOWN

So now that you two have been texting, how do you know if you want to take the next step? In this chapter, I will show you how to text him so that he asks you out on that first date. I will also cover everything you need to know to have a successful first date.

Everything You Need to
Know About Texting

Whether you are a big fan of texting or not, chances are that you text a lot. It has become a quick and easy way to communicate. When it comes to dating, texting can help push the relationship forward if used right, but it can also ruin a new romance. If you have exchanged numbers, but he hasn't asked you out yet, please keep in mind that you are texting towards the first date. That's it. You are not texting him because you are bored or to vent when your day isn't going well. You are not texting him to build a connection. Texting, especially at this stage when you guys haven't met in person yet, is nothing more than a tool for him to ask you out.

Texting isn't a real conversation and it doesn't create real bonding. If you think the more you text him, the more natural it will be in person when you do meet, you are looking at it wrong. Texting doesn't build up a relationship like hanging out in person does. It cannot substitute the necessary in-person time, talk, and activities you do together to know each other better.

Also, how your new match appears in texting may be vastly different from how he really is in person. It has happened to me multiple times when I was overly excited because my new match seemed fun and compatible with me through texting, but the moment we met in person, something felt off. So, if you want to save your precious time and find your love fast, don't text him too much before you even have met in person.

In order to ensure that texting pushes your new romance forward, your texts need to appear even better and more attractive compared to the messages you sent him in the dating app. This increased perceived value and attraction will make him have the urge to ask you out and get to know you more.

Remember the three rules for in-app messaging? Keep your messages short and sweet, match the intensity of his messages, and only respond at your convenience. These three rules still apply here, but they need an upgrade. Add some spice and flavor to your texts so they are more fun and pleasant to read. This way, by texting back and forth, he will automatically link you with the sweet and fun girl in his mind. If your personality is a little more sarcastic than fun, feel free to use that as your special flavor, but be careful as being sarcastic too early on may be misunderstood, especially over text.

If you are still confused about how to add spice and flavor to texting, simply be as fun and witty as possible, but also stay within your style. Give a little thought to your text and find the sweet spot. At this stage, texting is the only medium through which he can get to know you. Therefore, if you are interested in him, you want to spend some time thinking about what to text him back. Here are a couple ways to text him back if you just received his text for the first time.

Let's say he texts you "Hey this is Chris from Tinder." If your name is hard to pronounce, say something like "Hi Chris! If you are wondering how to pronounce my first name, I'll show you when we meet." If his area code is different from the city you guys live in, say something like "Hey you have a Florida number!" Or simply say "Awesome, you found me!" Don't just respond with a "Hey." That is boring and adds nothing to the conversation.

Also, take it up a notch by showing off your independent life while staying mysterious. What if he asks you whether you are doing anything fun tonight after work. Maybe you are excited to finish reading a book in this new coffee place, you are super ready to go hit the gym after sitting down all day, or you are about to go out with your friends. After you send out that vague and yet, joyfully independent text, he may wonder what book you are reading, what you look like in workout clothes, and who you are going out with. Guess what all these thoughts will make him do? Ask you out as soon as possible so he gets a hold of you!

Now, to double the chance of him asking you out, give him a hint. Some guys find it challenging to bluntly ask girls out when they are not sure what you would like to do as the first date. They may be hesitant to ask you out, even if they are super interested in you. You want to make it easier for him by giving him some hints. If you like coffee, say something like "I've been wanting to go check out the new coffee place on H street." If you have a favorite drink, text him "Just finished my run, a chocolate martini sounds super good right now." This way, he knows what you like to do and has a better idea of how to ask you out without being rejected.

What I can't emphasize enough is that you must be decisive in your response once he is committed to going on a date with you. If he texts "Do you wanna go grab a drink together or meet for coffee?" please don't say "Sounds good, you pick," or "I'm fine with either one." Take the lead and make a choice because that shows confidence and it affirms that you are happy to see him. Instead, say something like "Coffee sounds great! I know an awesome coffee place we should go check out."

What if he keeps texting you, but doesn't ask you out? Gradually lower his priority in the group of guys you text or message. Increase the time you take to text him back while decreasing the length of your texts. If he still doesn't upgrade his game, call him out. Say something like "Hey I've had fun texting you, but I'd prefer talking in person. I'm not one of those girls who like to text my time away," or "You really like texting, don't you!" If you feel bolder, try saying "You seem fun texting, but I wonder if you are as charming in person."

If you like him a lot and the text messages have been going smoothly, but he just doesn't pop the question about meeting for a date, say something like "So when are you gonna ask me out?" If he texts "You are fun, but I would like to get to know you more," say something like "Lol are you asking me out?" Some guys need a little more direction. Remember, your goal is to find your love as soon as possible, and the only way to do so is to delete those guys from your life who don't meet your standards. If he cannot step up his game to move the relationship from texting to meeting in person, he is out.

Before the First Date

Where to Go?

Romantic movies and relationship magazines make us think about a romantic candlelight dinner when it comes to a first date. But in the world of online dating, would you be comfortable staying throughout a long dinner with someone you've never met before? Early on in my dating history, I agreed to have dinner with my new match at a fancy steak place for our first date. He texted me, letting me know that he had arrived and grabbed a table. It all seemed romantic and promising until the moment I saw him. To be honest, I wanted to leave at that moment. To make it worse, after we ordered and were waiting for our main course, he started talking about how long it's been since he had a date and how depressed he was.

I was sitting there, speechless, watching this awkward guy half-crying in front of me. People at tables near us started looking our way. It was one of the worst moments in my entire dating experiences. If you don't want to be stuck in situations like this, consider meeting at places and restaurants where you can leave whenever you want. It can be grabbing a drink at a bar, having coffee together, or trying out a new ice cream place. To make the experience better, pick a place that you already like or somewhere you have been thinking about checking out. This way, even if the date doesn't go well, you will still have fun.

Another reason that you want to keep your first date short is that at such an early stage, your new date probably hasn't done anything to earn your time. As a woman, if you don't even know him but commit to spend so much time with him, you will come off as desperate and he won't see you as desirable. You need to keep dates shorter in these early days to keep your mystery and let him know you have other things going on in your life.

Also, don't feel compelled to agree to what he suggests. If you are not a big drinker, you don't have to agree to grabbing drinks with him. Say something like "I'm not a big drinker, how about ice cream?" If you don't like going to Starbucks and he suggested that for coffee, feel free to bring up a cafe you like. You want this experience to be as pleasant as possible, even if he or the date may not turn out to be pleasant. Bottom line is that you should meet somewhere in public for your first date; somewhere that you feel safe and comfortable.

When planning for the first date, try to be spontaneous and flexible if the original plan doesn't work out. For example, fifteen minutes before my now husband and I were supposed to meet for the first date, he texted me saying the place was closed for a private event. I was already on my way, so I texted him "Let's meet somewhere close by?" He responded "Sure." I checked what's around there and found another place I liked, so I responded with "Let's do Hard Rock Cafe!" Taking the lead and coming up with somewhere else if the original plan didn't work conveys confidence. Bonus points if you show positivity and passion when you bring it up.

Which Day to Pick?

I'm not saying you should go and see a psychic before setting the date so the relationship becomes promising because the stars were aligned. However, you should pick a weeknight for your first date, instead of the weekends. The reason is simple. On weekdays, you are already out and about for work, so you are more used to being around people. This will make it easier for you to go meet a stranger and have the most fun possible. Save the weekends for the second or the third date if he gets there.

As far as the time goes, don't start later than 7:30 in the evening on weekdays. Meetups later than 8:00 p.m. tend to have a sexual connotation. Also, have something fun or relaxing planned for yourself after meeting with him, such as watching a movie at home or catching up with your bestie. It doesn't have to be anything significant or important, but in case the date doesn't go well, you know you only have to be there for a bit and then you can go do whatever makes you happy. In cases when your date does go great and he asks you what you are doing after the date, your response will show that you have a fun life.

Communication Before the Date

Although this is just the start of a possible new romance, I want you to know that *you* are the one to decide how to communicate with him. If you prefer to talk with your new date over the phone before meeting up, don't be afraid to let him know that. Text him something like "I'll get off work at 6:00 p.m., feel free to give me a call then! (smiley face)." If you miss the good old days when texting didn't play such an important role in dating and guys had to ask girls out over the phone, be direct and let him know that with a quick message like "I like it when guys ask me out over the phone, the old-fashioned way, (smiley face)."

If you decide to talk to him over the phone, be sure to do it in a confident manner. If you are most confident having phone conversations standing up or walking around in your apartment, do it that way. If wearing your cozy pajamas makes you feel more lazy than confident, change into something else before the call. Don't forget to smile even though he can't see you, as you will sound more pleasing. Also, remember to keep the call under ten minutes and have something planned for yourself after the call. It will keep you from talking too long with him and reflect your enriched life in an attractive and mysterious manner. Don't let him think this call is the highlight of your entire day.

If you are more of a texting type of girl, pay attention to how much you text him before the date. Let's say today is Monday and you have agreed to meet up on Friday. You shouldn't text him every day until you meet, unless he texts you first. If he does text you every day, how much should you text him? Here is the rule of thumb: Put him on a lower priority level after you have set a date. If there is another guy you are chatting with on a dating app that you would like to meet but hasn't asked you out yet, focus more on sending him the right signals so he will ask you out.

At this moment, you shouldn't be the first to initiate the text if he doesn't text you. You've already committed your time to going on a date, and he hasn't earned any extra attention from you yet. Here is an exception: If today is Thursday and you two are supposed to meet up tomorrow but there hasn't been any communication in between, you can send him a text that says "Hey! Are we still on for tomorrow?" If he responds by saying "Yes, looking forward to it," don't respond back.

In my online dating experience, some guys texted me every day until we went out for the first time while others didn't text at all. Either way is completely normal, due to various personalities, and it doesn't indicate whether he is boyfriend material or not. In fact, when my husband first asked me out on Tinder, he didn't even text me after setting up the date. When I asked him after he became my boyfriend, he said he didn't feel the need to keep in touch because we already agreed on meeting up.

Getting Ready

How should you get ready for your first date? Are you having your eyebrows waxed, getting a matching manicure and pedicure, buying that new shade of makeup, splurging on the fancy dress you've seen while window shopping, and visiting your favorite hair salon? After all, it is the first date that you are getting ready for, right? No!

I understand that you may have a crush on your new date, so you have the urge to impress him by going out of your way to look your best. But, after all, he is just a stranger at this point.

While you do want to look good, you should spend more time on preparing your answers to this following cheat sheet.

A lot of times when we are on the first date, we get nervous and cannot express who we really are. The purpose of the cheat sheet is to prevent that from happening. Pick one question in each category that you feel like answering the most and feel free to come up with new questions if you don't like these or want more examples. Your answer to each answer should be composed of "what" and "why." Please remember that "why" is more important as it reflects the unique you.

1. Pick a book, movie, or videos that you have a strong feeling toward and the reasons. What was the most recent book you've read and why do you like or dislike it? What is your favorite movie and why do you like it the most? If you haven't watched a movie or read a book in a while, which one is the next on your list? Why are you excited to watch or read it? If there is a podcast or audiobooks that you listen to regularly, what is the reason behind it? If you are more of a YouTube or Twitch girl, what is your favorite channel and why?

2. Think of an experience that you have strong emotions about; happy and excited, or nervous and scared. What is the most exciting thing you've done in this past month? What was a new experience you have had most recently? When was the last time that you felt so nerv-

ous or scared and your heart was bouncing out of your chest? What is something that you are excited to try that you've never done before? Is there something that can bring up a smile every time you think about it? More importantly, what is the reason behind it?

3. Think about countries, cities, or even places in your city that you love. What was the best vacation you have taken or the best work trip you've been on recently and why was it so special? If there is a city or a store that is your happy place, what is it and why does it make you happy? What is your next trip that you are planning for and why is it exciting?

4. Is there a story that can best describe your personality? Do you have a story that you feel proud about and always have fun sharing? If you are spontaneous, brag about the last-minute trip you took. If you are goofy, talk about that time when you were the only one wearing a Halloween costume to class. If you like binge-watching shows, share about the long weekend that you spent three whole days relaxing at home finishing the entire six seasons of *Gossip Girl*. Don't be afraid that he might judge you or think any of your stories aren't good. It is your story, it is unique, and it is partly what makes you who you are now. That's more than enough.

5. Think of something exciting you are looking forward to, like a friends gathering next weekend, or a trip to another country in several months. This is something that makes you feel thrilled just thinking about it. It doesn't have to be anything big and require a lot of money. It could be as simple as making yourself a cup of authentic Hong Kong-style milk tea at home that coming weekend.

For all these cheat sheet questions, spend some time thinking about your answers. If you are comfortable with it, it is a good idea to share your answers with your best friend or simply talk about it out loud in front of a mirror. Again, make sure you reveal your "why" to the "what." It doesn't matter if your favorite book is *Freakonomics* or *Harry Potter*. What does matter is how reading *Harry Potter* makes you feel like a little kid every time you read it and how the world is magical and anything could happen. The reason behind "what" is priceless. Your facial expression, your body language, and how your eyes light up when you talk about these favorite things will help present who you are and will make you even more irresistible in his eyes.

First Date Really Isn't a Date

The Right Mindset

You and this handsome guy are meeting up for the first time this coming Friday. You have been so nervous and agitated about it. In fact, you keep thinking about it day and night. *Maybe he will be the one! He looks really hot from his picture! What if he doesn't like me? What if I embarrass myself by ordering the wrong drink?* You keep practicing each movement, from entering the bar to giving him a hug, and from what to say when ordering your drinks to how to play with your hair. *Does a hug seem too eager? Should I just do a handshake instead?* You keep talking to your friends and coworkers about this big first date you are about to have. It's driving you crazy because you cannot get your mind off it. Your heart beats so fast every time you think about the moment you two meet, but it's only Wednesday.

The truth is, you have never met him in person. He seems handsome, but there is so much more to a person than the look. You don't know how he carries himself. You've exchanged several texts or maybe texted here and there throughout the week. However, at the end of the day, he is still just a stranger. Don't get overly excited.

We call it "the first date," which sounds romantic, but really it is just a meetup. You two are meeting each other for the first time to see where the chemistry is, if there is any at all. The right mindset is to be calm and focus on having a great time. See it as a fun and unique experience where you get to know someone new. Afterward, you get to go back home to your comfort zone. However big this meetup seems to be right now, some day in the future it will be another funny or awkward story you can share with laughter.

Also, don't tell your coworkers or all of your friends about the date, unless they are your close friends that you share everything with. Sharing this with people who aren't super important to you will only build up your unreal expectations and create unnecessary agitation. You need to remember this is just a casual meetup, not anything big.

What to Wear for the First Date

What would you wear if you are about to meet an acquaintance or a friend that you haven't seen for a long time? You probably won't spend a crazy amount of time on your makeup or wear something super fancy, but you probably want to look presentable and stay on the better side of your daily look. Same goes here. Dress like how you normally would if you want to look nice, but not overdone. If you are going on a date after work, there is no need to change after work, unless your job requires you to wear a specific uniform and you change your clothes anyway.

When I went on the first date with my husband, I didn't go all out and wear an evening gown. I normally don't wear any makeup and in winter I like to wear a cute sweatshirt, a warm skirt, and long boots, so that's what I was wearing. Only after the date did I realize I forgot to wash my face that morning because I was running late! Oh, well. He was just a stranger at that time, and I didn't need to go an extra mile to look super nice for him when my time didn't allow.

What to do Before the First Date

If you took my advice and have a first date planned after work, make sure to get some quality work done that day, but don't be burned out from your overwhelming workload. If you normally work out before having dinner at night, get a quick workout in before meeting him. If you usually call your best friend on your way home from work, give her a call like you always do. Don't change anything that you normally do, but make an effort to spend the day in a self-disciplined and productive way. This will allow you to be in a better mindset and appear more confident during the date.

Also, don't act differently just because you are on a date. If you like taking pictures of the art-inspired cocktails you order, don't skip it because you are worried he may judge you. When I was arriving at Hard Rock Cafe to meet my now husband for the first time, I took a picture of the restaurant across the street. Guess what? When I sat down in the cafe, he asked me "Was that you that took a picture just now?" I was a bit embarrassed that he saw me, but hey, that was me! I like taking pictures, and I'm not going to change just because I am going on a date.

What to Say: Use These Expressions

If you have the correct mindset and prepared the cheat sheet, you are already halfway to having effortless conversations on the first date. Here are a couple of expressions to use to take it to another level. Only use them if your date is going on well and you would like to see him again.

1. "I love it!"

   When he mentions something that you would normally just say "That sounds nice," say "I love it!" instead. This phrase is full of passion and nobody can resist that.

2. "You look really good tonight."

   If you want him to ask you out again, you need to give him the right hints so he knows you like him. Pay attention. Don't say "I like your shirt," or even "You look good in that shirt." Guys are not the smartest creatures when it comes to compliments. You need to be straightforward. If you compliment his shirt, his mind goes "Wow! I guess this shirt is awesome. I'm gonna buy another six shirts like this!" Trust me, when he hears this, he will instantly like you more, and he will strive to look good for you every time he sees you.

3. "I'm so glad I met you!"

   Don't say it at the end of the date when you two are about to hug goodbye. Say it casually during the date instead. For example, when you are discussing a controversial movie and you share his opinion, say "I'm so glad I met you! I completely agree with that!" This phrase assures him that you enjoyed meeting him and will make sure that he knows you would like to see him again.

4. "We should do it together! I bet it'll be fun."

   Say this during the middle of a conversation when he talks about something that seems exciting to you. For example, if he says "Ice skating is full of fun! I always wanted to check out the ice rink at the National Gallery of Art. I heard it's beautiful," you say something like "We should do it together! I bet it'll be fun." This conveys that you want to see him again and sets up a plan for a future date.

Who Should Pay for The First Date?

Some dating experts say guys should pay for the first date while others prefer going Dutch and splitting the check. In my opinion, you should always offer to pay your part, but don't go out with the guy again if he doesn't insist on paying for you. If he says "I got it," or "I asked you out so I should pay for you," give him a big smile and say thank you. If he doesn't offer, you know you won't be seeing him again. Offering to pay for what you ordered is the basic etiquette for a lady, but paying for the meal that he invited you to is what a gentleman should do.

How to End a Date

When you are having fun on a date, it's hard to put a stop to it. Ideally, you want to keep it under two hours. You want to end the date on a high point so that he keeps asking you out. It's a good idea to wear a watch or set a timer on your phone to let it vibrate after 90 minutes or so. When you would like to end the date, say something like "Do you know what time it is?" Then say "Already? It's been fun! I have to get going though, I need to get some work done at home." Give him a generous big hug and say something like "Thank you so much for the coffee/drink, I've had a great time!"

If he leans forward to kiss you, playfully turn your head away so it lands on your cheek or your hair. Then look at him with a smile and say "Maybe next time." The reason that you don't want to give him a kiss already is because he hasn't worked hard enough to earn it yet. If he insists on walking you home or to your car, politely refuse him and say something like "It's very sweet of you, but maybe next time." It may be a sign that he is a sweet gentleman, but it's also possible that he may turn into a stalker. At this point, you don't want him to know where you live or your car license plate number.

After the First Date

If You've Had A Great Time

Let's say your date went great, and you can't wait to see him again. You get home and keep checking your phone for his text. You wish you could just text him how much fun you had! Here is my advice: Don't! If you have dropped hints during the date that you would like to see him again, now the ball is in his court if he wants to make a move.

However, when he does text you, don't let him wait for too long before you respond. Remember the texting rules I talked about? Keep your texts short and sweet, match his intensity, only respond to his message at your convenience, add spice and flavor to your texts, and stay mysterious while showing off your enriched independent life. These still apply here. If you liked the date a lot, it is especially important to restrain yourself from getting excited and shouting from the rooftops. If he texts "You looked really good tonight," don't respond with "You were so hot too! I wanted to rip your clothes off!"

Match his intensity and say something like "You were definitely handsome too!"

It is crucial to add value to the conversation when you respond. Don't let him do all the work of keeping the conversation alive. If he texts "I've had a great time tonight," don't just respond with "Me too!" The conversation would die. Instead, add value to the conversation and say "Me too! I've learned so much from you and thanks for the drink!" If he says "It was fun! We should do it again sometime soon," don't just say "I agree!" Instead, take the time and say "I agree! I really enjoyed our time together tonight."

Let's put this rule into a group of text messages. Notice the difference before and after the rule and watch how the magic happens.

Text messages between Quincy and Chris after their first date before applying this rule:

Chris: My face is so cold from being outside!

Quincy: Ya was definitely a cold night! (Matched his intensity, but didn't add value to the conversation.)

Chris: I had a great time. Do you still want to go ice skating this weekend?

Quincy: If you want to (Intensity not matched. She sounds uninterested.)

Chris: I do. Does this weekend work?

Quincy: Yup it should. (She let the conversation die again.)

After applying the rule of adding value to your text when you respond, it looks like this:

Chris: My face is so cold from being outside!

Quincy: Haha me too! The leftovers smell so nice lol (Matched his intensity, also added something else.)

Chris: Well I had a great time tonight!

Quincy: Me too! I've learned so much from you and thanks for the drinks! (Sweet, positive, and added value.)

Chris: Well would you like to go ice skat-ing this weekend?

Quincy: I'm too jammed this weekend, but next weekend sounds good! (Creates mystery. She has other things planned so she offers an alternative time. He knows she is definitely interested in meeting up again.)

Back when I was dating, I bought a book called *The Rules*. It says women need to keep men waiting for hours before texting them back, and girls should never text guys first. This was probably one of the biggest myths, in my experience. Following that advice will only make you seem uninterested and drive away good guys with confidence that don't wish to spend endless time begging for your attention. The key to staying in the sweet spot is to *NOT* wait for him to text you first all the time. If he texts you the same night after the date, feel free to text him first the next day. Relate your text to something you talked about on the date and keep it short. My husband and I talked about hot chocolate on our first date, so the next day I sent him a picture of hot chocolate made with protein powder and the caption "Look what I made!" This way, he knew that I was thinking about him and making that connection.

What If You Want to Leave the Moment You See Him?

One time, a date and I decided to meet at a metro station and walk to a bar together. I got there, looked around, and saw this guy whose face looked kinda like his picture. He walked all hunched over with his head down. The way he carried himself wasn't attractive at all. My brain went *Oh. My. God.* and my legs refused to walk toward him. For one second, I had the urge to text him "Sorry something came up and I couldn't make it." The only reason I didn't was because I thought about karma, and I know I wouldn't want to be stood up by somebody else.

If you don't believe in karma, of course you can run away if this ever happens to you. However, I encourage you to still go. Remember, you can always leave after 15–30 minutes! Forget for a second that it is a date and think of it as a work meeting. The truth is you never know what the conversation with this guy will lead to. Maybe he will talk about something you didn't know before, and there is nothing bad about learning something new. Just remember to tell him before you leave that it was a good talk, but you are not interested in seeing him again.

If you have decided that you don't want to see him again, be sure to let him know. A good guideline is to treat your date the way you would like to be treated. Tell him politely that it was nice hanging out with him, but you are not interested in meeting again. See the word "nice" here? This is not a mistake. I know I haven't recommended using this word in any texts or messages because it gives off a boring vibe. But in this case, we are rejecting him instead of impressing him, so feel free to throw this word in. It is a good neutral word that won't lead him on or crush his spirit.

Debating Whether He Scored a Second Date?

If the date was just mediocre, should you see him again? You should consider both how the date went and how he followed up with you afterward. What if the conversation wasn't too fun compared to another guy you met the same week, but he paid for the date, treated you right during the date, texted you saying he wanted to see you again, and you did have some chemistry with him? Give this poor guy another chance for a second date! If you think I am too nice, here are my reasons.

Some guys get really nervous when they meet you if they haven't been on many blind dates, especially if they find you extremely attractive. As long as you are somewhat attracted to him, give him another chance. Also, the more dates you go on, the less likely you will get hooked on one specific guy that you are most attracted to. Other guys you go on dates with will be able to pick up the vibe that you are popular among guys.

To be honest, I loved my husband's vibe the moment I saw him. However, as we sat down and started talking, it wasn't exciting at all. He seemed nervous and barely talked about himself. In fact, he showed me a funny video about an angry kangaroo fighting a man. Nevertheless, knowing that I was planning a trip to New Orleans, he gave me tips on where I should visit, and seemed genuinely into me throughout the conversation. He texted me right away afterward and asked me out again. I decided to give him another chance. To this day, I still remember the moment during the second date when my mind went from *I don't really care about this rando* to *Wow! he is actually fun and I find him sexy! I hope he wants to see me again!* After we got engaged, I made fun of his bad performance on the first date, and all he said was "I was way too nervous because I was really attracted to you. I didn't talk about myself because I wanted to know everything about you!"

What Are You Doing This Weekend?

"What are you doing this weekend?" is a question that you will get asked a lot during the early dating phase. This is him trying to find out possible date plans. It is crucial to answer it in the right way as it could boost your attractiveness, but it may also lower your perceived value if answered wrong.

Telling him all your detailed plans is going to murder your mystery. You may tell him more details later if he asks more about it, but keep it vague for now. If you are having a relaxed weekend with no plans made ahead of time, he doesn't have to know that either, as it may look like you have zero life outside of dating. I know some women would be bold and respond with "Going on a date with you?" This may be fun and witty after he is officially your boyfriend, but it goes beyond the intensity of his text for now. After all, he is asking about your plans this weekend, not actually asking you out.

Your answer should be vague but inviting. In other words, show your value but remain mysterious while making it easier for him to ask you out. (After all, you've only met him once!) Respond with something like "I have something planned here and there, what's up?" Saying this indicates that you have a fulfilled life, but you are not sharing too much. It also gives him room to ask you out that weekend. Once he actually asks you out, be decisive in your response. If he texts back "Well would you like to go check out the farmers market Saturday morning or we can grab lunch together." Don't say "You pick." Be decisive and convey your confidence and positivity. Say "I love farmers markets! Let's do that!"

The First Date

Before:

- ✓ Before you have met in person, keep your texts short and sweet, match the intensity of his text, but add some spice and flavor to it.

- ✓ Set the first date to be short on weekday nights and ensure your ability to leave when you want.

- ✓ You decide whether to communicate with him via phone call or texting.

- ✓ Prepare your answers to the cheat sheet before going on the first date.

- ✓ The right mindset for a first date is to be calm and focus on having a great time.

- ✓ Dress like how you normally would, but don't go overboard.

- ✓ Make an effort to spend the day in a self-disciplined and productive way and don't act differently because of the date.

During:

- ✓ Use these expressions if your date is going on well and you would like to see him again: "I love it," "You look really good tonight," "I'm so glad I met you," and "We should do it together! I bet it'll be fun."

- ✓ You should always offer to pay your part, but don't go out with the guy again if he doesn't insist on paying for you.

- ✓ Keep the first date under two hours.

After:

- If it went well, let him text you first, but don't always wait for him to initiate future text exchanges.

- If he asks you "What are you doing this weekend?" your answer should be vague and inviting.

Step 4

READY FOR A SECOND DATE... AND BEYOND?

"Dating has taught me what I want and don't want, who I am, and who I want to be."

—JENNIFER LOVE HEWITT

ow that you have finished the first date, time to dive into the second date and more! In this chapter, I will talk about the importance of making him infatuated with you in the first several weeks of dating and how to make it happen. I will illustrate the intricacies of the second date and unveil the foolproof third date guaranteed to make him want more. You will learn what you need to know about this guy by the end of the third date.

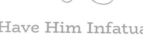

Have Him Infatuated
with You Now

Online dating is a part of our fast-paced digital life stuffed with information and endless distractions. He is probably communicating with several people on dating apps (as you should be too), so it is crucial to keep his attention and get him infatuated with you in the first few weeks of dating. Nobody will have the patience to know more about you if they don't feel a connection during the first two or three dates. Follow these three infallible guidelines to make him desire to know more about you even when it's only the second date.

Don't Be the Instant Noodle

Let's be honest, instant noodles don't taste that great. No matter how appealing the packaging looks, that brick of ramen noodles doesn't come close to the gourmet picture on the package. In addition to the bland taste, they are also high in calories and not filling. Yet, some people are hooked on instant noodles because they are convenient and cheap. They are ready to eat in three minutes and all you need to do is add boiling water. When you are exhausted and starving after a busy day, that doesn't sound too bad, does it? However, in dating, don't be the Instant Noodle.

We all know those Instant Noodle girls. These are girls that he never takes out for a date. She comes over to his place late at night to "Netflix and Chill," ordering takeout at the most. He gets to see her whenever he wants, at his convenience, and doesn't need to put in any effort to keep her around. She may feel that he likes her so much and cannot live without her, but at the end of the day, he will never see her as girlfriend material.

You are not one of them. You are an invaluable, attractive woman that deserves to be pursued by a good guy who respects you. You must not be easy. You must speak up when someone tries to treat you like a doormat. If he seems to always ask you out last minute, tell him as much as you would love to see him, you've already made plans tonight. If he asks you to come over to his place, tell him at this moment it's more fun to go out. Be the Michelin Gourmet, not his easy Instant Noodles.

Your Definition of "Cool" is Wrong

We think we need to be cool to have the upper hand in dating, especially during the early stages. Maybe this is because of misguided "dating secrets" or trying to emulate those popular, but distant, players. We have been taught that you put on a poker face on dates, nodding "That's fair," while screaming *Holy Shit! That's amazing!* inside your brain when your date says he's been to Antarctica.

You see your favorite dessert on the menu and cannot wait to order it, but you have to remain cool and decline by saying "I don't do dessert." In fact, refraining from expressing real emotions and feelings is not cool. It is boring. The real coolness showing emotions, being fun and passionate, and acting like a real human being instead of a robot. Go ahead and let him know you are impressed next time he shares his cliff diving experience. Tell him that tiramisu is your favorite dessert and you are going to order it! Be genuine and be real.

Be His Ally

Treat him as an ally although you have just started seeing him. When he asks you out and offers more than one idea, be the teammate and pick one instead of saying "It's up to you." When you both have arrived at the restaurant, only to see that it's closed for a private event, step up and come up with an alternative instead of waiting for him to do all the work. When he has paid for the baseball game tickets, take the lead and offer to pay for the hot dogs. You should definitely not be easy, but please treat him like your teammate on the same project, not your maid or your provider. You will be amazed how much he appreciates it.

The Second Date

Whether you are totally hooked and cannot wait to see him or you simply agreed to going out again to give him another chance, it's time to dive into the essentials of the second date.

Choose a Different Dating Dynamic

If you went to grab drinks on the first date and spent the entire time sitting, do something that requires physical activity this time. Check out an art gallery together, visit a local museum, or go visit a farmers market. You get the idea. Doing this will give you both a more thorough idea of what it's like to spend time with each other, especially if he is on the shy side and failed to impress you the first time. Engaging in activities together will take the pressure off him so you will have a better idea of how he genuinely wants to act around you.

Show Him More Sides of You

You probably didn't have a chance to show him all the fascinating sides of your personality on the first date. The second date is where you expose more of your personality while getting to know him better. I'm not saying you should go crazy and act completely different than you did on the first date, but just allow him to see other sides of you that he hasn't seen before. After all, we all have contrasting aspects of our personality.

If you told him on the first date that you work in a biochemistry lab doing research on cancer cells, let him know that you also play an instrument and perform at events from time to time. If you spent the majority of the first date sharing your passion for music festivals, reveal your nerdy side by explaining your Pokémon card collection. If you reveal something new about yourself each time, you continue to surprise him with your unknown sparkling qualities that will keep him wanting to know you more.

Divide the Date Into Two Parts

You want to divide the second date into two parts. The first part is what he thinks the date is, and the second part is what you keep to yourself. Let's say you've agreed on checking out a farmers market together. Scout out somewhere nearby that you guys can go afterward if the date is going well. It could be a board game bar or a cute bookstore. This way, you can learn more about him without possibly wasting your time. It will also make him feel that he has successfully impressed you and has earned the extra time with you. To make it happen, say "I just realized there is a board game bar nearby! Do you like playing board games?" It also demonstrates that you are spontaneous, and it is hard for guys to resist a spontaneous and fun girl.

Limit the second date to under four hours. If the connection is still going strong after the board game, it's OK to have a casual lunch together, but don't drag it out for too long. Let him know that you have other plans later during the day.

Avoid These Activities

A popular idea for a second date is watching a movie together. You haven't known each other long enough to be able to comfortably stare at a screen in silence together. Also, you are supposed to use a second date to get to know more about each other. It is hard to make that happen by not talking at all.

Watching a movie together, even in a public cinema, is overly romantic. Sitting in a dark theatre can easily send out a misleading message that you two are in a romantic or intimate relationship, which isn't the case. After all, you have only met him once before. Watching a movie lying closely beside each other in the dark gives him the idea that you are comfortable with that level of intimacy, which isn't what a self-respecting woman, like yourself, should do. Admit it or not, it sometimes makes us feel lonely when we are surrounded by couples that hold hands or lean against each other. Giving off a lonely vibe at such an early stage in dating should be avoided at all costs.

Another danger zone that you should absolutely stay away from is "come over and cook." When a guy invites you over, it's implied he wants to get physical with you. Unless short-term sex is what you are looking for (in which case you should stop reading this book immediately), it is in your best interest to not get physical this early. Second date, and even third date, should be done in public. It is better for your safety and it conveys that you are not one of those girls that goes over to a guy's place when you barely know them. If he invites you over, simply say something like "I have to admit that I like you, but I'm not one of those girls who would come over this fast." If he fades away? Congratulations! You have just saved yourself some trouble in the future.

Who Should Pay?

Same as the first date: Offer to pay for your part, but ideally, he should pay for you. However, if your second date went beyond the first part, you should pay for something small in the second part. If he pays for your boba tea and pastries at the market, it is your turn to pay for a drink at the board game bar. If he pays at both the farmers market and the board game bar, take the lead and pay for lunch afterward. In cases where he insists on paying, don't fight with him over that. Simply let him pay and say thank you.

Follow-up Text

If he has done an excellent job treating you right during the second date, send him a positive follow-up text afterward. Be sure to let him know that you had a great time and refer to a cute moment of your time together. Say something like "Hey I had a great time! Have to confess that I kinda feel bad crushing you at the board game though (winky face)," or "Hey I had a great time! Thanks for not laughing at my 'awesome' board game skill (palm face)."

After sending the follow-up text, let him text you first for most of the days, but take the initiative to text him first sometimes. Do we need to go over the texting rules again? I told you I was going to repeat this several times! Keep your texts short and sweet, match the intensity of his texts, only respond to his texts at your convenience, add spice and flavor to your texts, stay mysterious while showing off your fulfilled independent life, and always add value to the conversation.

Second Date Red Flags

A major red flag on the second date is if he comes across too eager, too fast. I once went on a first date with a seemingly sweet guy. I received this text right after the first date: "I'm so happy I found you! Please let me know when you got home." The following days he kept texting me like we were already in a relationship. Although it seemed odd, I thought maybe he really liked me!

I told him I was catching a train to New York at 5:00 the next morning. Surprisingly, he offered to drive me to the train station, even though it required him to get up two hours before my train. Back then, I had only met two people from online dating, so what he did wasn't alarming to me. Instead, I was excited that I may have found someone special! After all, he was so sweet and considerate. He even planned to walk me to the turnstile, so he would know that I made it safely. I barely got any sleep that night as I was excited to see him.

What really happened, however, was much different from my expectations. He tried kissing me as soon as he saw me outside of my apartment and seemed disappointed when I turned my head away. I was in shock because he hadn't even touched my hand yet. Once I got into his car, he put his hand on my lap when driving. I wasn't comfortable with it at all, but I didn't say anything. I was afraid that he might think I didn't like him. Throughout the drive, he gradually moved his hand toward my upper inner thigh, and I had to stop him before it became too inappropriate for me. I politely told him that I was attracted to him, but he was making me uncomfortable.

He moved his hand back to the steering wheel and said in a cool voice, "Oh, OK." Neither of us said anything after that. I was sitting nervously in awkward silence, hoping to get out of the car soon. He didn't even leave the car to give me a hug at the train station. I had a feeling that I messed it up. I kept checking my phone in agitation, but I never received any texts from him. Sad and confused, I started blaming myself in tears. *Why did I refuse his kiss? Why did I move his hand away?* Eventually I decided to text him explaining myself, hoping things could go back as they were, but his lack of response completely ruined my visit.

I thought he broke my heart. Fast forward five years. Now that I look back, I could see clearly that it was a major red flag. If a guy gets too physical with you this early and ghosts away after you politely decline him, it is a red flag that he isn't looking for anything serious. Don't blame yourself or cry like I did. Go celebrate because you dodged a bullet with this guy whose real purpose was solely to get into your pants. In fact, for your own safety, don't put yourself in a position where you have no control, such as getting into his car when you barely know him. Remember the rules I've already outlined.

Should You See Him Again?

After the second date, pay attention to how you feel when you think about him. Are you excited to see him soon or are you not sure whether to go out with him again? If you keep telling yourself how great he is, but for some reason still feel the need to justify dating him, it is probably not a good sign. If you need to tell your best friends how amazing he is and subconsciously want them to persuade you to go see him again, clearly you don't feel strong chemistry with him. In this case, you probably shouldn't see him again. Simply let him know that you don't feel you two are a good match, and thank him for treating you with kindness and sincerity.

If you are dating two people at the same time and feel more chemistry toward one of them, don't stop seeing the other guy just yet. In this scenario, keep dating both of them and you will be able to make a decision later with more information and more confidence.

The Third Date

The Foolproof Third Date That Makes Him Want More

If you and your new match have made it to the third date, it means that you two have passed the "complete stranger period." Chances are that you have been talking with each other for a while now and things may be heading to the next stage. Therefore, it is crucial to have a third date that will definitely make him ask for more dates with you if you want to see him again too.

The third date should be active and engaging. An ideal third date is going out for a run together or hiking in a mountainous park. If you both work long hours or have a long commute, it's perfectly fine to schedule it during the weekend. However, if you have just met him on the weekend, you want to get the momentum going and have the third date during the middle of the week. In this case, engage in dopamine-releasing activities that can be done during a weekday night. If it's cold outside, go bowling together, find an indoor go-karting place, check out a local Topgolf, or practice Bikram yoga together. If it's warm and bright outside after work, go for a short outdoor run together, hit balls at the batting cages, or explore an easy weekday hiking trail.

What to Wear

Another secret to an unforgettable third date is to wear something athletic. Show him your sporty side that he has never seen before. Tie your hair in a messy bun or an easy ponytail, wear your yoga pants or athletic leggings, and put on your favorite tank top or a tight-fitting sports top. You are definitely going to take your attractiveness and sexiness to another level and make it hard for him to not ask you out again. It also lets him see a more down-to-earth side of you.

You Decide What to Do

Don't be afraid to speak up about what you would like to do for the third date. If he asks you out again, take the lead and suggest "Let's go for a run together!" Guys are usually expected to be the one to set up dates, so taking the pressure off him by coming up with an idea once in a while will make him like you even more. If he has already suggested a plan that isn't exciting, like dinner and a movie, feel free to say something like "I was thinking about something more active!

Let's go for a hike on a trail!" Trust me, you will blow him away with your confidence and active lifestyle.

Don't Overthink

If you are self-conscious about whether you are a good runner or you haven't bowled for years, don't worry about it. If you are not confident about how your body looks in sports attire, you are not alone. We all have insecurities, even supermodels. The key is to take part in an activity together that will get both of your heart rates up, while showing off the active and sporty side of you. The easiest way to let your worries and concerns go is by focusing solely on experiencing the present moment and having fun.

What You Need to Know by the Third Date

You can be secretly thrilled to go on a third date with the same guy, but it is still important not to get overly excited. There are plenty of things you need to know by the end of this date, which requires you to watch and listen to him carefully during it.

If you still have no clue what he is looking for from online dating yet, make sure to ask him. By this point, you need to know whether you two are on the same page. Is he up for a relationship if things flow that way, or does he just want someone to hang out with? Does he plan to get married one day or has he made it clear that he doesn't believe in marriage? It is vital to be clear about his intention before you let yourself completely fall for him.

If he asks the question "You seem so amazing, but why are you single?" don't be automatically offended. This question is framed as a semi-compliment. You may assume that he is implying that there is a negative connotation to being "still single," but he may be saying that you are so great and you should have been married by now. Before answering it, be sure to clear up this faulty background assumption first. Tell him that you are too picky. Say something like "I love my life as it is. I like the idea of a relationship, but it has to be with someone right. I just haven't met someone that special yet."

Also, be aware if he says he is moving away in the near future. If he casually brings up that his company is sending him away to Russia for a year, you probably don't want to keep seeing him. A long-distance relationship requires a substantial amount and time, energy, and money. It is better to avoid it at such an early stage as it is hard to really connect when you aren't able to date in person.

By the third date, people tend to get more comfortable with their relatively not-so-new date, so they will speak and act with less restraint. The third date is when you should start getting to know him on a deeper level. Watch and listen very carefully to him and see whether he checks the major boxes of being your potential boyfriend.

1. **Listen to what he says and determine whether it meets your boyfriend requirement.**

   If you want your future boyfriend to be a family guy, he had better check that box. If he says he isn't a big fan of Thanksgiving because it forces him to spend time with his parents, make sure to ask more about it. If he wasn't joking, it is a clear sign that he isn't qualified boyfriend material for you.

2. **Watch how he reacts when things don't go as planned.**

   If there is an unexpected long wait at Topgolf, observe how he deals with the unpleasant moment and how he treats the staff there. Does he give them a hard time for something that's not their fault? If this behavior bothers you now, just know that he won't change in the future.

3. **Watch how he treats you if you are not experienced in the activity you are doing.**

   What if you are going ice skating but you are not very good at it? Does he offer to hold your hands and encourage you along the way or does he make fun of you? I was once on a date with someone that I had seen for a couple of times. He always opened doors for me and even brought me flowers occasionally. I thought he was truly a gentleman until we went ice skating together. The moment he realized I wasn't very graceful on ice, he pushed me out of nowhere and I immediately fell down. When I told him how unacceptable it was, he simply laughed and thought it was fun. All the fun we had and all of the charisma I thought he had disappeared immediately. There was no way I could allow someone like this to be my future boyfriend.

Who Should Pay

If he refused to let you pay for anything the first two dates, you should definitely insist on paying this time. Otherwise, he may think you are taking him for granted and no guys want to be treated that way. If you paid for some part of the second date, do the same this time. Don't feel pressured to pay for the main part of this date.

Are You Supposed to Kiss Now?

One of the biggest misconceptions about online dating is when the first kiss should happen. In my opinion, it is up to you when you want the kiss to happen. There is no hard and fast rule. Generally, you don't want to be the one leaning forward to plant the kiss. However, you can make it happen by giving him appropriate hints. After a hot and steamy third date (of physical activity!) where you've both got the heart rate up, I recommend two ways to make the kiss happen, depending on how liberal or old-fashioned you are.

The first method is on the bolder side. If you are positive that you both have mutual desire for the kiss, wait for that romantically intense silent moment when the date is about to end. Look into his eyes, smile and playfully say "so when are you going to kiss me?" After that, don't say anything, just wait for him to have an epiphany and go in for the kiss. What's important, however, is to keep the kiss short. Make sure to nonverbally convey that this is just a quick kiss and there is no room for more.

The second method is what I am personally more comfortable with. If you are happy with how the date went, hug him at the end while kissing him on the cheek. Doing so implies that he has gained the permission to kiss you from there. You may leave him confused, but most likely he will kiss you next time. Don't worry about him taking this as rejection, as your texting interaction later will clear up his potential misunderstanding.

If you don't feel ready to kiss him yet, don't kiss! Remember: YOU are in control. Being the genuine you is the best way to ensure he likes you for who you really are.

Texting Afterwards

If you sent him a follow-up text after the last date, allow him to text you first. Otherwise, it will come off as too desperate, especially if you hinted at kissing. If you two have already had the first kiss, use texting to build up the sexual desire. I'm not saying send him a nude picture, but simply send him something like "Just thought about how you kissed me yesterday, it was so hot." If you kissed him on the cheek, say "Just thought about the kiss last night, can't wait for a real one next time (winky face)." This text will create sexual tension and allow him to see you as sexy without actually having sex.

Texting at this point is becoming more casual, but it doesn't mean you can do it the way you text your best friend. Remember the key rules and let him text you first most of the time, but be the first to text him once in a while.

Be a "Player"

When I hear the word "player," I imagine an attractive guy with a smirk on his face. Charming, but dangerous. Nearly all of us have dealt with at least one player. If not, you probably have heard your friend complaining in tears. She thought she was his only girl, but soon realized only that she was merely one of a club.

Here, however, I am using the word "player" in a different way. I'm not asking you to be girlfriend of more than one guy at a time or to sleep with so many people that if you were to get pregnant, you wouldn't know which guy was the dad. "Be a player" here means to date two to three guys simultaneously at this stage. You may be particularly interested in only one of them, but you have fun and have some chemistry with the other two. I know you are busy, and you only care about that one guy in particular, but hold the skepticism and let me explain.

When we are hooked on only one guy, we have the tendency to give him too much attention. We check the phone for his texts all day. More often than not, we read between lines and overanalyze the relationship. We respond to his messages immediately, no matter if we are in the shower or taking a nap. We get super excited to see him again. We have the tendency to be exceedingly available to him. As guys, they can sense it! They know if we are always here waiting for them to come to us. They know we will happily go out with them as long as he asks, even though it's last minute or even though he doesn't give you enough attention. It is exactly the opposite from what a confident girl would do—what you should do.

On the contrary, dating three guys at the same time allows you to have a fuller life, if you don't already, and be less available than you otherwise would be. You get to compare how three different guys treat you on and in between dates, and which guy you really prefer. It makes you less likely to fall for one specific guy when it is still too early to make a rational decision. Trust me, if you have fallen head over heels for someone after going out with him three times, it is too early.

More often than not, the guy that you like the most right now won't be the one that you find most charming in a month. Plus, when you do get bored and find yourself waiting for one specific guy's message, talking to all three people at the same time would make you less likely to go crazy. It prevents you from seeming desperate when he finally texts you and lets you get to know the other two guys a bit better.

You may be thinking it's hard enough to finally meet one guy that I have chemistry with, let alone three! So how do you get three? I admit that it is hard. Sometimes you need to go out with nine different men in order to find three guys that you are happy to keep seeing. A lot of times you go on three first dates in a row, but you don't want to see any of them again. This is why dating at this stage is all about dating hard and having fun. Your goal should be to go on three dates per week, or at least two.

Dating three guys at the same time means that you haven't become official with anyone yet. If any of them asks you to be his girlfriend and you have agreed, you must stop contacting the other two guys. Otherwise you would become a real player, in the worst sense of the word. Admittedly, it is not likely that they ask you to be their girlfriend at such an early stage. Really, you still probably don't know them well enough to make it official just yet.

Second Date

Before

- Make him infatuated to you in the first few weeks. Speak up when treated like a doormat, be genuine and real, and treat him like a teammate.

- Choose a different dating dynamic, show him more sides of you, and divide the second date into two parts.

- Avoid watching a movie together or "come over and cook" for the second date.

During

- Offer to pay for your part, but ideally, he should pay for you.

- Keep your second date within four hours.

After

- If it went well, text him that you had a great time and refer to a cute moment of your time together.

- A major red flag is if he comes off too eager, too fast.

- After the second date, pay attention to how you feel when you think about him. It will tell you whether you should see him again.

Third Date

Before

- To make him want to see you more, the third date should be something fun and engaging in activities that release dopamine.
- Wear something athletic. Show him your sporty side that he has never seen before.
- Don't be afraid to speak up for what you would like to do for the third date.

During

- The easiest way to let insecurities go is by focusing solely on experiencing the present moment and having fun.
- By the third date, you need to know whether you two are on the same page, whether he can check major boxes of your ideal future boyfriend, and whether you want to see him again or not.
- If he refused to let you pay for anything on the first two dates, you should definitely insist on paying this time.
- It is up to you when you want him to kiss you.

After

- Texting at this point is becoming more casual, but it doesn't mean you chat away like you do with your best friend.
- Date two to three guys simultaneously at this stage.

Step 5

DATE SMART AND
ASK QUESTIONS

*"Love is everywhere. Follow your heart
but take your brain with you."*

— ALFRED ADLER

*L*et's say you've gone on more than three dates with someone and you both still want to know each other more. Congratulations! It is definitely exciting to finally get to this stage. I'm sure you've gone out with plenty of guys and you've eliminated many from the game. Exciting as it is, it's also one of the most crucial stages. Are you going to have a high-quality boyfriend that treats you right? You are in control.

In this chapter, you are going to figure out whether he is genuinely interested in you in a serious way, and determine if he can be one of the right candidates to be your amazing boyfriend. If so, how much should you involve him in your life?

Who Is He?

You have to answer this question correctly in order for this potential relationship to bloom beautifully. Who is he? Is he "your guy" already? Not yet. He is just one of the guys that you've gone out with four or five times. He may be a bit special in the sense that you like spending time with him and want to know him better. But, at the end of day, he is still nobody. Don't act like you are his girlfriend already. In fact, he has barely made it to your heart yet.

How much you involve him in your life can directly affect whether he treats you like a prize worth earning in the future. This ranges from how often you text each other, to letting him meet your friends and colleagues. The rule of thumb is to match his level of communication and interest. If he texts you at least once a day, be the first to send him a fun text some days. If he invites you to a housewarming party to meet his friends, bring him to a happy hour party that your friend is hosting. This way, you avoid coming off too desperate but also assure him that you are attracted. If he hasn't already introduced you to any of his coworkers or friends, don't show up at a work event with him. It will make you seem more eager and give him the upper hand. If you would like to meet some of his friends, communicate this to him instead.

The most important thing is to be honest with yourself and understand who he really is to you at this moment. Even though you may involve him in your life at that perfect level, you will still be deceiving yourself if deep down you believe he is more important than he really is at this point. If you keep reminding yourself that he is only someone you started seeing recently, you will naturally give him the right amount of attention. You will keep your options open both on and offline. You will be more aware of it when someone is trying to flirt with you. If you are mentally hooked on him, however, you are more likely to shut down your "social valve" and choose to stay in your comfort zone simply because you think you already have someone.

Is He Genuinely Interested in You?

When we really like someone, we have a tendency to focus on how great he is but overlook whether he is interested in us in a genuine and serious way. A guy's actions speak louder than his voice. Pay attention to these three areas and you will have a clear idea on how much he values you.

1. He is consistent in communicating with you in between dates.

    Guys that are genuinely interested have you on their mind. They feel the need to talk to you at least once a day, even at early stages of dating. He wants to hear how your day went. After you have seen each other for a longer time, he is going to be more forward and want to have a real conversation with you on a daily basis. In contrast, guys interested in a short and casual relationship tend to vanish in between dates. You have a great time in person, but afterward, you barely hear from him. After not contacting you for days, he asks you out again without feeling the need to explain anything and disappear afterward. Their hot and cold behavior drives you crazy.

2. He makes an effort to see you.

    Think about the dates you have been on. Does he make plans to see you at least two days ahead of time, or does he text you asking if you are available tonight? Do you normally hang out in his neighborhood, or does he travel to you from time to time? Do you need to take public transportation and walk in the rain to meet him somewhere far away, or does he pick you up at your convenience? Does he make an effort to plan fun and romantic dates, or do you eat take out and watch a movie together? A high-quality guy that wants a serious relationship with you will do everything he can to impress you and go the extra mile.

3. Drop hints and then watch whether he picks up on them with his action.

This won't apply unless you have already been on four or five dates together. For instance, if you don't have a car but you need to go somewhere far away, let him know and see if he offers a ride.

Before my husband and I started dating exclusively, I was seeing another guy at the same time. Back then, my ID card was expiring but the Department of Motor Vehicles was a nightmare to reach by public transportation. Every time I joked with my now husband that I was going to drink with an expired ID, he would offer to drive me there. I said the same thing to another guy who also had a car, but he laughed at it every single time without offering to drive.

Another idea is to tell him something that's bothering you and see if he provides any solution. Back when my husband and I were dating nonexclusively, I was hosting an Airbnb. I needed to make sure the apartment was cleaned professionally before guests arrived. One day, the cleaning service cancelled on me last minute. I told both guys about this and my future husband offered to come over and help me clean, whereas the other guy simply provided some emotional comfort and started bragging how great his day went.

Another time I was using a paperclip to hold my keys together after my keychain broke. It kept falling apart and I nearly lost all my keys. Hearing that, my future husband immediately said, "I'm going to get you a key ring." The next time we went out, he brought a key ring and even put them on for me.

I'm not saying that you have to be passive-aggressive and expect a guy to read your mind and know what you want. I've already explained that you need to stand up for yourself and be decisive. But, casually hinting about an issue is a good way to see how he responds. Girls tend to pay attention to sweet talk rather than actions. Instead of being intoxicated by what he says, open your eyes widely to watch what he does. Guys are natural fixers. They are born with the instinct to fix the problems for people they love and to make their lives easier. If he keeps texting sweet things but never offers real help when you need it, delete his number and move on.

Five Questions to Ask

When we fall head over heels for someone that we haven't known for a long time, we are likely to focus on the parts that we know and like about him and gloss over parts we are unsure about. In other words, we have a tendency to idealize guys that we like. If you know that he loves his dog to pieces, you probably think he will be a good daddy, even though he may never want a baby. If you see how he helps his buddies, you may assume that he offers the same level of support when his parents need an extra hand, when in fact he couldn't care less about them.

In order to know him in a well-rounded way, here is a list of questions that you can refer to and weave into conversation when you are out on a date with him. Be sure to prepare for your answers in case he asks you back. Information sharing is a two-way street. While you are trying to figure out if he is good enough for you, he is also thinking about whether you are right for him.

1. What is his career goal? Is he working toward it?
    If he currently works as a manager but he wants to be a regional manager, what is he working on to get there? You don't necessarily need to understand his field, but he

needs to have a plan. If he is a bartender and he doesn't have other ambitions, will you be OK with it?

2. Does his job hinder his ability to have a relationship?

If he is a commercial consultant and travels 200 days per year, will you be able to handle a perpetual long-distance relationship? If he is active duty military, he will move around constantly as part of his career. Would you be willing to uproot and move to keep the relationship going?

3. Does he want to settle down in the foreseeable future?

This question takes more technique to ask compared with others. Instead of asking him directly, listen when he talks about his career goals. If he admits that he is still exploring different career options or thinking about travelling around the world to find his niche, you know he won't settle down for a while. If he sees building his new business as the top priority, but you would like to have a family within three years, you know that he is not the best candidate.

4. What about kids?

This is another question that you may not be able to ask bluntly. Try this: If you have a little niece who you love to hang out with, tell him about her next time he asks about your weekend. Watch his facial expression and listen to his reaction when you say "I love that little girl so much! She brings me a ton of joy!" Does he go "Awww" and tell you how little kids melt his heart, or does he leave it at "That's nice"? If he replies with "Wow, good for you, I can't stand kids. Thank God I don't have to deal with them ever," you can take that as a clear sign that he doesn't want kids.

5. How is his relationship with his family?
He may have already told you stories or jokes of his family, especially if he is serious about you. If he never talks about them, don't be afraid to bring it up. I once dated a guy for a month that I thought was charming and handsome, until one day he told me his mom is from another country. He had this condescending face and went "She is just a foreigner and doesn't really understand me, so I keep my distance from her." All the good feelings I had toward him disappeared the moment I heard it. If he doesn't even respect the woman that gave him his life, how would you expect him to treat you, or your mom, when you guys are together?

The key to asking these questions is to be confident when bringing them up. If you are concerned whether you should ask any of these because you are scared it may push him away, it is probably a sign that he isn't treating you fairly anyway or maybe you aren't ready for a real relationship. Trust me, if anything, having the courage to ask these sets you apart from the majority of women that casually date. He will see you as someone special, because many women are a little unconfident and don't communicate so directly.

Pull Him Closer

If you are still attracted after asking the five questions, and if he continues to show affection, let me show you how to pull him closer. It is important to know that what I'm about to share *only* applies after you've gone on around six or seven dates or have been dating for about a month. In other words, if he asks you to be official at this point, it won't be too much of a surprise. This disclaimer is extremely important as you should not do these things early on, otherwise they make you seem desperate.

1. Compliment him with details.

    Guys love to be complimented as much as women do. By now, you should have complimented his appearance a few times. It's time to deepen the compliments to another level. After you go grocery shopping together and he helps you put your vegetables in the fridge, lean into him and tell him "Thanks for putting the food away for me. I really like how considerate you are!" When he holds your hands in public, tell him "I really like holding hands with you. It makes me feel safe." When he picks you up and opens the door for you, tell him "Thank you for always treating me like a lady. You are such a gentleman." Guess what these specific compliments will do? They will make him like you even more, and they will make him want to keep being considerate, helping you feel safe, and being a gentleman for you. When it comes to compliments, guys are like little kids. The more specific the compliments are, the more likely he is going to act that way in the future.

2. Ask his opinion.

Guys love it when women ask their opinion on things. It makes them feel important and respected. If you are looking to buy a new car or a new laptop, ask his opinion on it. He will feel like you value his experience and viewpoint. It's going to make him subconsciously think of you as someone more important, compared to other girls that he is casually seeing. Also, this gives you an opportunity to see how much he values you and your needs. After sharing his opinion, don't forget to sneak in another compliment. "You are so brilliant! I totally overlooked it before you mentioned it."

3. **Let him know he can be vulnerable.**

    If he opens up to you or allows himself to be vulnerable in front of you, grab the opportunity and respond in a way that makes him feel safe and comfortable to do so. If he tells you that his day didn't go too well, give him a hug and tell him "Aw, I'm so sorry you had to go through it. You are being very strong and you are doing a great job." This way, he knows he can be vulnerable with you, and thus will be comfortable to share more with you. A guy seeing you as his future girlfriend largely depends on whether he feels comfortable showing you his vulnerable side.

4. **Take advantage of texting.**

    When you text him, be generous and focus on giving him emotional support. If he says he is going to have a challenging day at work, text him "Good morning, handsome! Good luck with your meeting today at work! I know you are going to be amazing!" If he responds to you saying "Aww thank you! Your message makes me feel much better," say something like "Great! Now I'm even happier!" In this example, your texts provide emotional value and will make him feel better. That's the only purpose of your text. You are not looking for validation or reciprocation.

    Another way to push the relationship forward by texting

is acknowledging what he did and pay him a compliment via text. If he came out of his car to open the door for you and give you a kiss, the next day text him "Just thought of how you kissed me before opening the door for me last night, it was so hot." If he always takes care of driving, navigating, ordering, and paying when you are out on dates, text him "I really like how protective and chivalrous you are every time we go out." These texts will keep you on his mind when you are not together and will make him miss you even more. They also show that you aren't taking him for granted and you appreciate and recognize his efforts.

5. Share with him what you want in life.

Tell him there is a dream future that you are working toward and getting married is part of it. If you would like to have kids in the future, it is important to let him know as well. If it scares him away either because he doesn't want kids or he thinks it is too much to talk about, go celebrate, because you've eliminated a wrong guy from your life. If he is one of the right guys for you, sharing this will make you seem even more irresistible. Who doesn't like a woman that has her life together and has a goal to pursue?

6. Convey your standards.

Let's be honest, it can be challenging to call someone out if he is not treating you the best. To make things worse, it's even harder if you are attracted to him. However, conveying your standards to a guy in the right way can actually make him see you differently. This will separate you from other girls.

When you are communicating your standards, be sure to make it firm and yet positive; no nagging or whining allowed. If he keeps showing up late to your dates, instead of saying "OMG you are late again!" go with "Hey I see that you are late a lot. I value my time and your time when we plan to meet up. I prefer my man to be punctual." If he always expects to see you in his part of town and doesn't offer you a ride, instead of texting him "You lazy butt! Why always your part of the town?" say something like "Do you mind if we do something closer to my neighborhood?" If he usually texts you to plan a date last minute, don't say "Do you really think I will go out with you when you ask me this late?" Instead, text back with "I already have plans tonight, but it would be great if you wanna take me out on a date Friday night!"

Another advantage of conveying your standards is that it sometimes naturally leads to the next question: What are we doing now? For example, I was dating this guy for almost two months. Everything was fun and exciting. However, I went on a work trip to Seattle for three days and this guy disappeared the entire time I was out of town. The day after I came back, he texted me asking how my trip was. I immediately told him I was surprised how he vanished for three days, because things have been going great between us. I thought we were getting serious about each other! He was surprised and said we never talked about what we were doing. Then he told me he wasn't ready for a serious relationship and thought we were keeping it casual. Good thing I told him my expectation!

How Physical Should You Get?

I am aware that "sex on the third date" may be the norm in American dating culture, but it doesn't mean you should follow it. I suggest you only have sex with him after you are in a committed and promising relationship. You may not want to hear this, but I know it will benefit you greatly in the long run. He will see you as someone with high standards, and that is different from most women out there. Although it is extremely hard to resist the urge to jump your sexy date, it will save you from potential heartbreak if he turns out to be not worth it.

Although sex is off the table, it doesn't mean you can't get hot and heavy. It is OK to kiss him passionately. He is allowed to kiss your upper shoulder area and your neck. You can even let him touch you with clothes on. Things can still get wild making out. However, since you guys are not official yet, keep your clothes on. If he asks you about it, say that "I am really attracted to you, but I won't get physical unless I know we are in a meaningful relationship."

Say this directly and confidently and see his response. If he is genuinely interested in having a serious relationship with you, he will respect you and wait for you to be ready. If he gets frustrated, emotional, accuses you of being ridiculous, or pressures you, you know he doesn't respect you. In this case, he is definitely not the right guy that you should get into a relationship with. After all, the quickest way to find your Mr. Right is to delete the wrong ones from your life as soon as they reveal themselves.

Red Flags and the Right Responses

Pay great attention now because if you heed these warnings, you will save your future self a lot of time and tears. When you spot these red flags, please don't try to make excuses for him or justify sketchy behavior.

1. He is not physically close to you in public.
    Of course, he doesn't have to wrap his arm around you
    or hold your hands walking down the street, since you
    are not official yet. However, if he keeps a distance from
    you in public but gets intimate with you privately, it
    is a red flag. Guys that are genuinely interested in you
    naturally want to be close to you, in public or not. They
    are proud to be seen with you. They have an innate urge
    to shout out to everyone that "Look! I'm dating this
    beautiful lady!"

Players, however, tend to stand next to you with some
distance in between, such as walking down the road, in
a grocery store, or waiting in lines getting movie tickets. They don't want people they know to think that you
are dating each other. If you aren't sure if he is a player
or just shy, let him know how this makes you feel. Say
something like "I love it when you hold my hands when
we hang out at home. I miss that when we are out in
public." If he comes up with excuses and doesn't work
on changing this behavior, gradually lower his priority
in your heart compared to other men that you are seeing.
Sometimes, he may just not be an affectionate person. If
you are looking for more affection, look somewhere else.

2. He doesn't communicate consistently
   between dates.

A boyfriend-material guy that is sincerely interested in you will communicate consistently in between dates. If he says he thinks about you all the time, but just doesn't like being on the phone, that is a straight up lie. We are in an era where almost everyone brings the phone every-where. If he asks you out consistently and shows you affection when you meet, but you barely hear from him in between dates, it is either because he is emotionally unavailable, he has a wife and maybe kids, or he has a real girlfriend. Tell him how you like your time together, but you want more communication. If he gives excuses and doesn't make more of an effort, save your future self some time and tears and lower his priority in your mind.

3. He constantly pays you minimum "investment."

This is similar to the last scenario, but worse! This is a guy that invests in you so minimally that it is just enough to keep you hanging and believing that he likes you. You see each other once every two weeks or even less. You would like to see him more, but you just cannot get a hold of him. You are the one who constantly texts him first while waiting for days to get a response.

When you finally realize he is just not that into you and reluctantly decide to give up, he texts you out of nowhere with "Miss you." Your heart melts and your brain tells you *Yes he definitely likes me!* After you respond "Miss you too," he sends you something like "What are you doing next Friday?" Then, he disappears again for another week.

When you call him out and say "Hey, stranger. You always disappear on me," he may respond right away and text "Sorry I've been super busy with work, but let's do something next weekend." Guess what? He gets your hopes up again but next weekend passes by and you still don't hear from him about meeting up.

What you need to do is take a step back and stop feeding his ego. Lower the intensity of your text when he finally shows up again. Instead of saying "miss you too," say "That's sweet, thanks!" When he asks you what you are doing during the weekend, say "Some plans here and there, what's up?" If his sudden ghosting and flaky pattern continues, say this to him the next time he texts you: "It's getting old interacting with you like this. I like you, but the way you make plans, then disappear, then asks me out again, then disappear gets old. It is not for me. I'm not interested anymore." Don't fear that you are being too harsh on him. You don't want to be with someone who doesn't even invest in you at the very beginning. Remember your worth and don't let yourself get sucked into a relationship at his convenience.

4. He always leaves you waiting.

He says he is picking you up at 7:00 p.m. after helping his sister, then texts you at 7:30 p.m. that he is on his way. Eventually you get a text saying he is hanging out with some friends and will pick you up soon. Is this the way he treats the prize he worked hard for and values? I don't think so, and it isn't how you should allow yourself to be treated either. Remember: You are in control.

Tell him "You really like to keep me waiting, don't you? I'm excited to see you, but there are other things I'd like to do if we are not meeting today." If this keeps happening, tell him "Time is precious to me. I respect my time and others' time, and I expect the same from you." If you think it isn't too bad compared to other red flags, I hope you still agree that he is not treating you as a priority. What should you do when you are not treated like a priority? Lower his priority on your part too.

5. He doesn't remember what he said.

Maybe he keeps raving about a steak place that he wants to take you to, but never really takes the action. When you bring it up, he acts like he has never said that. If it happens occasionally, it won't be too much of a red flag. But if there is a pattern, be very cautious. It probably means he is seeing way too many people at the same time and you are not special enough. In this case, don't be afraid to call him out directly by asking "Have you been busy recently? It seems that you keep forgetting what you said."

When this becomes a pattern and gets even worse, like he says one thing and tries to convince you he never said it, it's called "gaslighting." Some guys like to play mind games and make you feel like you are stupid or forgetful. Do not participate in this kind of relationship. This is a major red flag and the sign of a manipulative and controlling person.

6. He is emotionally abusive.
    Emotional abuse is more subtle than physical abuse, but it is just as detrimental. Emotional abuse can take many forms. The most straightforward example is if they call you terrible names or say hurtful things to you. If they keep doing it knowing you don't like it, it is a bad sign. Another sign is if they constantly belittle you. What if you take up painting as a new hobby and proudly show him the new art piece you did, but all he says is it could be better? What If you reached your highest sales record at work, but he makes fun of you for thinking it as a big deal? Maybe you had a long day at work and complain to him about how tired you are. Instead of comforting you, he loses his temper and says he is hundred times more tired than you are and what you experience at work is barely worth mentioning.

Another serious sign is if he controls you. I have a friend whose husband banned her from wearing a ring that her parents gave her after he proposed. He thinks that she belongs to him. She is not allowed to go out and see friends without his approval. Many times, this kind of emotional abuse and control can turn into physical abuse and violence.

The last most common sign of emotionally abuse is if he acts super sweet one second and unleashes his anger completely on you the next. Some days he is the sweetest boyfriend ever, and other days he loses his temper arguing with you while driving like he is going to kill you both. Some days he thinks you are the best girlfriend ever and other days everything is your fault. He may be the most loving person one moment and then he yells at you out of nowhere just because he cannot find his nail clipper. If he acts like any of these, please leave him. If you think it's cruel for you to leave him, it is another sign that you've fallen his manipulative trap. If you don't leave him now because you think that will hurt him, you will be hurt a hundred times more later. Remember, he will not change and you cannot fix him.

7. He insists on getting physical.

I said earlier that no sex is allowed until you are in a committed and promising relationship. If he insists on getting more physical than what you are comfortable with, let him know. "Look, I really like you, but I don't feel comfortable having sex before we are in a committed relationship." Don't fall for it if he tries to pressure you by making you feel guilty or if he gets super sweet all of a sudden and even says "I love you," just to get in your pants. Keep your standards high so you are able to screen out all the guys who aren't worth your time. That's the only way to find your true love as fast as possible. Pressuring a woman for sex is a big red flag and reveals his true intentions.

Who Should Pay for The Following Dates

By now you should have a good idea about his job and financial situation. If you are in an industry or position that is likely to make more money than he does, you want to pay slightly more often than you would with a different guy. However, if you find yourself constantly paying and he seldom offers, it is a red flag. Guys are naturally providers and protectors. If they are good boyfriend material and really like you, they will try to provide for you to show their affection. Even though you make more than he does, no guy will feel comfortable letting the woman that he likes take care of the bills most of the time.

If he makes more money, the ratio of money spent between him and you should be close to 3:1. For every $30 he pays, you should pay $10. Don't pull out a calculator every time the bill arrives, but just have a vague idea in your mind. When a guy is treating you well in all other areas, the more he invests in you financially shows that he is serious about you and there is a better chance that you will start a relationship that's headed toward marriage.

What should you do if he expects you to pay as often as he does? If he paid for dinner last time and doesn't take out his card when the check comes this time, ask him if he minds splitting the check. Text him afterward something like "Sorry I had to split the check last night. I like eating out with you, but I am not making enough money to spend like that." If he is a good guy who really likes you, he will probably say "It's OK. I should have paid it anyway." Tell him you will try to step in within your financial ability, and that you definitely don't take him for granted. To a high-quality guy, it makes a difference when the girl makes an effort to pay something, shows appreciation, and doesn't take him for granted.

Recap

- He is just someone you've started seeing recently, not your boyfriend.
- Pay attention to his actions, rather than just his words, in order to have a clear idea on how much he values you.
- Ask him the five questions to get to know him better.
- Follow the six ways to pull him closer.
- Only have sex after you are in a committed and promising relationship.
- Pay attention to the seven red flags and react appropriately. Trust your gut instinct.
- If you make more money than he does, pay slightly more often than you would with a guy who makes more money than you do. If he makes more money, the ratio of money paid between him and you should be close to 3:1.

STEP UP YOUR EVERYDAY LIFE

"There is only one corner of the universe you can be certain of improving, and that's your own self. "

— ALDOUS HUXLEY

y goal is to help you find an amazing boyfriend online, but it's going to happen a lot faster if you expand these practices to your daily life during the same time. In this chapter, you are going to learn how to step up your game in your daily life, and how to "market" yourself on social media.

Step Up Your Game Offline

When you have two or three dates every week, you are likely to become more comfortable socializing with people in general. I would recommend that you take advantage of this and use it to accelerate the dating process and improve your social skills. These are four ways to step up your game offline in your daily life.

1. Have more small conversations with people throughout the day.

    Try to limit your time spent on the phone when you are out and about. When you wait in line getting coffee, start a small conversation with people standing behind you. It doesn't matter if it's a woman or a guy.

    Doing this will make you more approachable. Most of us women think it is a guy's job to approach us. However, it's extremely hard for guys to approach us, especially if we are on our phone, or if we don't seem approachable. By talking to those around us with a happy vibe, we are making it easier for guys to come up to talk to us.

    If you do this on a daily basis, gradually you will be able to start a conversation with someone that you are interested in knowing. If you fear that being the first to initiate a conversation will make you appear easy, it won't. You will actually come off as confident and easygoing. Believe it or not, guys appreciate it when women talk to them first. By doing so, you are giving them permission to talk to you.

2. Take your hobbies to a more sociable version.

   If you like painting, attend a painting class instead of doing it by yourself at home. If you would like to learn a new language, join a language class instead of trying to learn it online. If working out is your thing, join a fitness group class instead of hitting the gym all the time by yourself. Look for Google meetup groups and activities that interest you.

3. Host a "friends gathering" on a biweekly or monthly basis.

   I'm sure there is someone you know that you find attractive but haven't had a chance to hang out together. Inviting them along with your close friends will create opportunities for them to get to know you and you will come off as a gracious and popular host. Reach out in a confident and fun way: "Hey! We're all getting together for drinks this Friday night, you should come! Bring your friends!" It is hard to turn down such a confident and casual happy hour invite. Plus, most people secretly enjoy being invited to happy hours because it makes them feel like they are being included and they can meet people without the added pressure of an actual date. The key here is not to give specific attention to any one guy that night, and definitely don't get drunk or go home with anyone other than your roommate.

4. Don't pass up a chance to connect with a guy you spot in daily life.

When I was trying to have a boyfriend, I followed tons of dating experts. They encourage girls to send subtle hints to guys that we find attractive, giving men the "look" with a perfect smirk. I found that impossible to carry out. My smirk either appeared too weak and they barely noticed it or it came off as being insane.

What I found possible was to start a conversation. If you are on a metro, move closer and ask him for directions. If you are in a coffee shop, find a seat close to him and ask him the Wi-Fi password. If you are in a bar, walk toward him and ask what he's drinking. If you follow the first three suggestions on a regular basis, this one won't be too challenging.

Just remember, everyone is busy focusing on their own life and nobody is really paying attention to you. If anything, you will appear brave and confident to go after what you like and what you want. Worse comes to worst, this will just become another funny story someday in the future. However, in situations where you share mutual attraction, your move will make a difference for the rest of your lives.

I have put together a free 28-Day "Get More Dates Plan." You will know exactly what to do each day in order to date more attractive guys. Simply follow the guide and watch as guys in your everyday life become attracted to you like a magnet. Take action now by going to this URL: https://getdatesnow.ck.page/getdatesnow

"Market" Yourself on Social Media

Nowadays, almost everyone is on social media, mostly Facebook or Instagram. It is more important than you think to have your social media work toward a successful dating life and not against you.

Your profile picture should clearly show your face, with a big and confident smile.

Make sure your posts can reflect your fulfilled life. Post the trip that you made recently, snap a picture of you reading at a cute coffee shop, and share pictures of you dressed up with friends at concerts.

Whenever you are out with friends, and you have taken the time to look cute and dress beautifully, have them take pictures for you. Pick the best ones and post them on your social media. This could be challenging if you are camera shy. In this case, take some group pictures with your friends and make sure to look cute in them. Doing this regularly will make you get comfortable dressing up and posing for pictures, which will encourage you to embrace your feminine side.

Stay away from posting overly sexy pictures and barhopping posts. I'm sure you are going to get a lot of "likes" if you post these things, but potential boyfriend-material guys will see you as the opposite of serious girlfriend material. Your social media platform is your name card in today's world. Make sure your Instagram page reflects you positively and shows your cheerful traits and interests.

Recap

- ✅ Follow the four suggestions to step up your game offline. Your social media platform should reflect your high value as you are in person.
- ✅ Download the free 28-day "Get More Dates Plan."

Step 7

HAVE HIM BECOME
YOUR BOYFRIEND

*"Men may have discovered fire, but women
discovered how to play with it."*

–SEX AND THE CITY

ow that you've been on several dates and learned more about each other, what exactly are you at this point? Isn't that the eternal question in a dating relationship? Are you boyfriend-girlfriend? Casual dating friends? Are you headed toward a serious relationship? In this chapter, we will talk about becoming an official couple, making sure that is what you want, and when is a right moment to have sex.

Do You Really Want to be His Girlfriend?

Before we dive in assuming you would like him to be your boyfriend, ask yourself a question: Do you really want to be his girlfriend? This question is comprised of three parts.

First, do you like him? Is it really attraction that you are feeling, or is it familiarity and comfort? In other words, are you genuinely interested in seeing him, or you simply find it easy to hang out with someone that you have already developed comfort with? You need to decide if you are truly attracted to him or trying to make yourself believe that he is "the one."

This can be an easy question if you really like him. If, however, you find yourself needing to find reasons to convince yourself to move forward, it is a bad sign. If you are debating because he has all the great things on paper, but you feel reluctant to kiss him, it is a bad sign. I know you have already spent more than a month going out with him and things have progressed from nervous to familiar and comfortable. However, it shouldn't be the reason for you to become his girlfriend. Attraction is one of the most important factors when it comes to a long-lasting relationship. You need to be honest with yourself if you are not physically attracted to him and he deserves to find a woman who truly feels this for him. You are going to thank yourself later.

The second question you need to ask yourself is: Do you want to have him as your boyfriend because you think it can fix all the problems you currently have? A lot of women are not happy with their single life. They don't think they are beautiful enough, they constantly need validation, and they get lonely because they don't feel love from within. In these cases, they believe as long as they have a boyfriend, there will be someone out there constantly giving them validation. They believe after a boyfriend enters their life, they won't be lonely anymore.

A boyfriend is someone to provide you with more love and will make your amazing life even better. He won't be able to fix all your problems, and you shouldn't count on that. These insecurities can only be fixed from within. Loving yourself, having innate confidence, and living your life to the fullest is your own responsibility. Putting this responsibility on your future boyfriend's shoulders might feel easy at first, but it is going to slowly eat away the relationship and make it less stable. A boyfriend should only enhance your own happiness. He cannot be responsible for making you happy. If you don't work on yourself, you will become that super needy girl who turns into a burden rather than a strong woman who creates happiness within herself. That confidence and self-worth makes any woman irresistible.

Finally, is he really worth the space in your life? Is life with him truly better than your single life? Pay attention to how you feel when you are with him compared to when you are by yourself. Are you usually excited to see him? Does spending time with him energize you? Or do you need a lot of time to decompress by being alone after hanging out with him? Does being with him make you happy, or does it make you more emotional and less rooted? Do you feel yourself in a healthier position both physically and mentally after being with him, or does the relationship come with drama or constant second guessing? A relationship needs effort from both people to thrive. If being with this guy seems like a lot of work, or you feel yourself forcing it, it probably isn't a good match.

He Hasn't Asked You to be Official Yet?

You've been seeing him for a month or two now. You text each other throughout the day. You go out like a real couple. However, when your friends ask whether you are currently with someone, you don't know how to answer that, because honestly, you don't know if he is your boyfriend yet. He hasn't asked and you never brought it up. You are always looking for signs from him and waiting for him to ask you to be official, but you simply cannot get the courage to bring it up to him.

Maybe you are confused whether guys in today's world still ask that question anymore. You are afraid it would make you seem desperate to bring it up, and you don't want this "vague relationship" with him to end. At the end of the day, if he asks you to be his girlfriend, you would jump up and down with joy and happily scream out "Yes!!" with no hesitation. If this is the case, I'm going to show you how you can make it happen now.

Dating and sex have become a lot more casual these days, but some basic things don't change. In most cultures, if he is serious about you and he wants to move things forward with you, he will ask you to be official. The idea that you are not his girlfriend and somebody else may sweep you away is scary for him. If he hasn't asked you to be official, chances are that he is not ready yet. However, it doesn't mean you can't approach the subject without seeming desperate.

> How to bring it up:
  Before you actually say anything to him, remember, it's not so much what you say, but how you say it that matters. The way to bring it up has to include two parts: The first part is positivity and appreciation for the time you spent together, and the second part is raising the question in a calm and confident way.

> When to bring it up:

The best time to say it is toward the end of a date. For example, you say something like "I've really enjoyed spending time with you for the past two months and I feel that we are getting closer. Where do you think this is going?" Say it in a calm and confident way and be prepared for his response.

> After bringing it up:

Stay calm when you hear his answer. If it isn't the answer you hoped for, let your actions speak for you and refrain from responding with harsh words and a mean attitude.

He's Not 100% Ready for a Relationship?

> The worst reaction he can have is something like "Oh I am not ready for a relationship. I thought we were just having fun!"

In this case, don't show him your disappointment by responding with "I've told you that I want to get married one day! I can't believe you were just wasting my time!" Remember, your aggressive verbal reaction at this moment isn't going to make the situation work for you. Counterintuitive as it may seem, what you should do at this moment is to look like he was overreacting. Say this with a smile: "Relax! I just wanted to know what you think about it. I wasn't asking you to be my husband!" Then give him a big, sexy kiss. Afterward, pretend that nothing happened, carry on with the date, and kiss him goodbye since the date was going to end anyway.

The key point is how you treat him afterward. Make sure to lower him on your priority list. Give more priority to your family, your friends, and other guys you are dating. When he texts you, don't text him back unless you have finished all other things you need to do. If he asks when he can see you next, set a date at least a week into the future, and say sorry that you are busy with your friends or your job. The bottom line is that your actions need to convey that he is losing the priority in your life now that you know he isn't ready for a relationship.

Even if he tries to step up his game, he isn't as important anymore. He told you his true feelings. After all, your dating goal is to find a future husband. Remember the principle that we talked about in the first chapter? "No matter how attracted you might be to certain guys you meet during the journey, you must delete them from your life if they don't contribute to this end goal."

If you still think there's a chance this could work out and want to keep seeing him, make sure that everything about you is amped up a bit the next time you go out with him. Let him notice and remember how charming, fun, and spontaneous you are. Also, you need to end the date earlier than you usually would. Tell him that you have to go home earlier because there is something you need to work on. His mind is going to think *She is so sexy and charming! I'd love to spend more time with her, but clearly, she isn't allowing me!* Keep the pattern going, and he will eventually decide whether he wants to be in a relationship with you or he is just not that into you at the end of the day. If he cannot contribute to your goal of finding a lifelong partner, get rid of him from your life.

> The second worst reaction from him can be something like "I like how this is going, but I think we should know each other a little better."

In this case, he is not completely denying that there's a possibility of proceeding into a relationship, but he is being vague. You can say "I like how it's going too! But I had to ask because there are other people asking me. I would like to hear what you think before I give them my answer." By saying this, you are suggesting that you have other suitors and implying that he needs to step up his game. If he says something like "I do like you a lot, but I think you should do whatever you think is best for you," he means that he does like you, but he doesn't like you enough to fear losing you.

Again, no matter how much you feel the urge to react or cry, what he needs is space. You need to keep calm and give him the space to decide if he is OK with you ending up with some other guy. Simply let him know gracefully where you stand by saying something like "I like you a lot too, but I am ready for a relationship, so I don't think we are gonna work if you cannot decide by the end of the month," (give him around two weeks' time). Afterward, go about your life and treat him the same as the first scenario.

> The next response is where he is kind of ready, but still responds with a touch of vagueness: "I really like you, and I would like to date you exclusively."

This is still vague! You will end up asking your girlfriends "What does dating exclusively mean! Does he think I am his girlfriend now?" Ask him straightforwardly with a playful smile "So are you asking me to be your girl-friend?" See his response. If he gets serious and pops the girlfriend question, that's the action you want! If he approaches your playfulness with a joke or any type of avoidance, lower his priority in your heart according to the first scenario.

What's important is that all of these conversations need to happen face-to-face, preferably toward the end of a date, when both of you are sober. Having this discussion via texting will seem easier but is actually going to make it more complicated. You won't see how he truly reacts and even though you two had the conversation via text, the next time you see each other, it's still unclear where your relationship is heading.

> What if he asks you first "I'm curious, are you dating other people at the same time?"

Depending on how comfortable or playful you are, you can say "Are you asking because you don't want me to?" or "Yes I am, because you didn't ask me to be official yet." Remember, how you say it plays a much bigger role than what you say. Say it with your smile and confidence. Act like nothing has happened and be the hottest YOU possible after giving your answer. He is going to decide how he wants to go about it.

> What if he asks you to be his girlfriend, but you are not ready yet? Here is an example that happened to me.

When my husband and I went on the sixth date, we were sitting at the restaurant, excited for dinner to arrive. All of a sudden, he said, "I really like you! I would like to get this official." I might have looked calm and all together, but inside my brain was probably a nuclear bomb. My mind went *OMG are you kidding me? We've only seen each other six times!!* I didn't want to reject him, so I said, "I really like you too, but I think I need more time. Can I tell you later?"

After two weeks, I finally decided to say "yes." We were

walking down the street and I casually said, "So when are you going to ask me to be your girlfriend?" He went silent for a second and burst out loudly, "I did!" I said, "Can you ask again?" He looked at me all surprised and asked, "Does it mean you are ready now?" I looked at him and said, "Yes." He kissed me.

It's important to know that you absolutely have no obligation to agree to be his girlfriend the first time he asks. Give yourself plenty of time to think about it, based on what you've learned in this section. When you are ready, simply pop that question playfully and seal the deal.

Is It Really Official?

Most times when guys ask you to be official, they really mean it. However, sometimes you may think it's clear that you are his girlfriend, but something happens that makes you doubt it. Here are four signs that either the relationship you have with him isn't really official or isn't a long-lasting relationship. Watch out for these if you are in doubt.

1. Watch how he introduces you.

    Back when I was still new to dating, I was with a guy that I had been dating for two months. Things were progress-

ing nicely, but he never asked me to be his girlfriend. One night I came home from seeing a friend who had asked me if this guy was my boyfriend. I texted him right away "So my friend was asking me who was the guy that I went to the concert with." He responded with "Well, 'your boyfriend' has a nice ring to it." I texted back "Does it mean you think you are my boyfriend already?" He answered affirmatively.

The next time I saw him, he assured me that we were indeed official. Two days later, we went out to a basketball game and ran into one of his coworkers on the metro. He introduced me as his friend. Immediately, my mind went *Uh-oh! He didn't introduce me as his girlfriend!* I confronted him on it later and he simply said he forgot. Being kind and innocent, I believed him. Only later did I find out that he never meant it. Looking back, he also had plenty of other red flags, so I now see we were never going to start a promising relationship.

2. Have you met his friends or family yet?
    If his family doesn't live locally, has he mentioned you to his close family members? Most times the guy that sees you as his girlfriend cannot wait to show you off. They arrange happy hours and double dates so you can meet their friends or families. In some cultures, however, guys don't introduce you to their parents unless you are already engaged. In these cases, watch if he lets you meet his siblings or close friends.

The day after my husband and I became official, he attended one of the concerts I was performing in, and asked to have a picture with me. He sent the picture to his parents right away and posted it on Facebook. He also invited me to have dinner with one of his closest friends living in the area the following week. Trust me, when guys are really serious about you and are a hundred percent in a promising relationship with you, you will know it.

If your guy doesn't give you obvious signs, and you still don't know if his family knows about you, watch how he reacts when a family member or close friend calls when you are with him. If he says "I'm hanging out with a friend," or "I'm just by myself," that gives you a crystal clear idea that he doesn't really see you as his girlfriend, unfortunately.

3. Watch how he treats your family and friends.

If your family is coming to visit you from out of town, see if he acts like your man and helps you host them. If your friend is looking for a job in his field, see if he happily helps them polish their resume or passes along job opportunities. If he wants a long-lasting relationship with you, he will treat people important to you with great care and respect.

Two months after my husband and I became official, my parents came to visit from overseas. He helped me come up with a detailed travel plan for my parents and even invited them to Florida, where his parents live, for a short stay. I still remember that the moment he brought up the idea, I knew that my parents were important to him. That moment made me see even more that our relationship was really heading somewhere great.

4. If he is invited to a wedding, does he ask you to "save the date" ahead of time?

People usually send out "save the date" notices far in advance so that you can mark your calendar and attend their wedding. If he is invited to a wedding and can bring a plus one, he will want to ask you if you would like to come with him.

The month that my husband and I became an official couple, he was invited to his cousin's wedding. The same day that he received the "save the date" card in the mail, he asked if I could attend the wedding with him. Even though the wedding was four months away, his action meant that he had me in his mind going forward.

He Hasn't Put a Ring on It, Yet.

A common mistake that women tend to make is to start getting too comfortable and not acting like a "prize" months after becoming a girlfriend. He worked hard to pursue you and finally got you as his girlfriend, but that doesn't mean he has earned the right to marry you.

In order for the relationship to keep heading toward the next stage in a positive way, it is vital to continue keeping yourself as your top priority and act like a reward. He needs to feel that you are not "his" and if he doesn't keep up his game, he may lose you some day. I'm not saying that you need to dress overly sexually and flirt with other guys so that he feels the urge to give you that engagement ring, but there are things you should focus on in order to keep the relationship heading in the right direction.

The first and most important thing is to keep taking yourself to the next level. Remember how you attracted him in the first place? Whatever it was, whatever you did that made yourself irresistible in his eyes, keep on doing those things. If it's working out, going out for brunch with friends, learning salsa dancing, or visiting the Language Corner to learn a new language, keep focusing on self-improvement. Whether you have a passion for baking or solo travelling, keep doing those things that give you joy and make you super attractive in the first place.

I know it's much easier to snuggle up with him at home during the weekend when you would normally be going out for a run, but don't lose yourself in the comfort of a relationship. Learning new things will keep him surprised when he thought he knew everything about you. It will also keep the relationship fun and fresh. You can probably find things that you could both learn together too.

Be bolder when you compliment him. Now that you are officially a couple, enjoy the privilege of paying him bold and sexy compliments. If he came to help charge your car when your battery died, instead of saying "Thank you so much for saving me again," tell him "You are such a lifesaver! I'm so lucky you are my man." When his suggestions really helped you, say "It's so amazing that you can be so hot and reliable, but also extremely smart. It is so rare. I am so lucky to be your girl."

Stay away from moving in together. You may roll your eyes and say I'm too old-fashioned, but hear me out. In my opinion, moving in together is a scam. Movies and magazines make you feel that moving in with your boyfriend means that your relationship is moving to the next level; a level that is super close to getting engaged. However, in real life, moving in together is one or more steps further away from getting that diamond ring.

It is very likely you will get too comfortable with each other if you already live together. It will be hard for you to keep a bit of mystery and still enjoy your hobbies, if he is with you most of the time during the day. Also, if he already gets all that he wants when you move in together, what would be his incentive to marry you? Let me ask you a question: If you can go to your favorite supermarket and take whatever you want there for free, would you ever feel the need to buy anything there? The analogy might be a bit too extreme, but you get the idea. Old-timers often used the phrase "Why buy the cow when the milk is free?"

If you are worried about what it is really like to live with him without moving in, there are other ways to have a taste of that. Take some long-distance trips together. Spending long weekends together is another good idea. It is also acceptable to spend some of the weekday nights together. The bottom line is that you must have your own place, instead of official-ly living together. The risk and downside of moving in with him is not worth the tiny benefit that can be achieved in other ways. Plus, moving in together creates an unnecessary finan-cial dependence upon each other at this stage. If the situation goes south, then moving out, finding a new place, or break-ing a lease are all problems that may seem insurmountable if you decide to break up. Breaking up or living together should not be a decision based on finances.

For guys today, they naturally think there is a "move in" phase. Therefore, tell him that you are not one of the girls that move in together before marriage when he brings it up, even if it comes up in a casual conversation.

Sex Department Isn't Available During the "Probation Period"

Again, I am well aware that having sex with your match on the third date is the norm in American dating culture. However, that doesn't mean you should follow it. In fact, you should do the exact opposite if you are reading this. You want to find a great boyfriend that is going to be your husband in the near future. You want to avoid any possible potential heartbreak or time wasted. In order for it to happen, you shouldn't be having real sex with him until two to three months into the relationship, or later if that is part of your religion or culture. You might be calling me crazy conservative right now, but I assure you this is the right way to go. Doing so is going to help you find a great boyfriend that will later become an amazing husband while minimizing your chance of being hurt.

I keep emphasizing the importance of acting like an asset that he needs to work hard to earn. Being able to have sex with you will be one of the most marvelous things he will earn from you. Requiring him to wait for something this special is absolutely normal. Even most jobs require a probation period!

It is worth mentioning that two to three months isn't a fixed number. It is an estimated timeframe you need to feel out the relationship with him. You need this time to figure out whether he is the right person that you desire a promising and long-lasting relationship with, and potentially be excited to marry someday.

Saving your intimacy with him is also going to save yourself potential heartbreak. Let's say you are in a relationship with your new boyfriend, but only one month into the relationship you find out he is actually a habitual liar, which you (or anyone) absolutely cannot and should not tolerate. Not having sex with him will make it much easier for you to break up and get over him.

However, no sex doesn't mean no sexual tension. Remember when you were younger and weren't allowed to have sex? I bet you still had lots of fun making out with the guy you were with back in the day. Nowadays, we get to sex too soon, too early. As a result, good old making out gradually loses its position in today's dating life. It is actually a pity.

You are still able to do almost any other sexual activity with him, just not going all the way. As time goes by and you are more certain that you want to be with him in the long term, turn up the sexual heat a bit more. After you both are fully in agreement that you would like to potentially marry, go ahead and reward yourselves with that all-out sex that you both have been waiting for. I personally did it with my husband three and a half months after we got official. This was after the moment that I realized I loved him and I would like to marry him someday.

It's important to share your thoughts with him ahead of time. Before it starts to get hot and steamy, tell him something like "I find you smoking hot, and I cannot wait for the day to come. But I need to make sure our relationship is heading somewhere meaningful before I feel comfortable having sex with you." See how he reacts and continue with "I'm sorry for turning you on and leaving you hanging. I still want to provide you with everything you need in a relationship, including sexual needs. So before I feel comfortable, I want you to tell me if you are struggling with not having sex; that way we can talk about it more."

Having a conversation about sex in a mature way will help you understand each other more, which will in turn pull you closer. It will also make the two of you more comfortable talking about rough topics, which is crucial for a relationship to move successfully toward a great marriage.

Recap

- Check in with yourself whether you really want him to be your boyfriend.

- Bring up the "What are we doing?" conversation using two factors: positivity and appreciation regarding the time you spent together, and raise the question in a calm and confident way.

- Bring up the question toward the end of a date.

- Stay calm when you hear his answer. If it isn't ideal, let your actions speak.

- If he isn't 100 percent ready for a relationship, lower his priority in your heart. When he finally gets to see you again, make sure to come across as even more charming. End the date sooner than you normally had been.

- Remember the four aspects that give you a clear idea whether he truly sees you as his girlfriend.

- Keep leveling up. Keep learning new things. Be bolder when you compliment him. Do not move in together with him.

- Give yourself two to three months to feel out the relationship with him. Don't have until you are fully certain that he is the one you would like to potentially marry.

Step 8

HOW TO BOUNCE
BACK GRACEFULLY

*"Someday, someone will walk into your life and make you
realize why it never worked out with anyone else."*

—SHON MEHTA

inding true love isn't easy. If you are not the luckiest girl on the entire planet, chances are that you are probably going to have your heart broken a couple times before you meet your Mr. Right. Dealing with a breakup is one of the most brutal life experiences. It is something you need to get over on your own. In this chapter, I am going to talk about situations where you should consider breaking things off and how to bounce back gracefully after you do.

Cheaters Are Always Going to Cheat

If at any time during the relationship that you find out he has cheated before on his past girlfriends, save your future self some trouble and get out of the relationship. If you discover that he has slept with someone else after he got official with you, or even sexted with another girl after he became your boyfriend, break up with him. Once a cheater, always a cheater. Don't even try to imagine the fantasy idea that you are going to be the magic woman that puts an end to this handsome cheater's disloyal journey.

I once hosted a housewarming party where my friend Joshua brought his friend, Chandler. From what I had heard, Chandler had cheated multiple times before on his ex-girlfriends and even his current girlfriend, Celine. She knew all about them. She wasn't able to come to the party and Chandler arrived with Celine's brother. The entire night, Chandler was trying to flirt with Sandy, a girlfriend of mine who is smoking hot. He tried putting his hand on her lap multiple times in front of Celine's brother. Sandy later told me that three of them shared an Uber, and Chandler kept trying to invite Sandy up to his apartment. Again, this was all in front of Celine's brother. I'm sure Celine knows all the times that Chandler has cheated before, but I doubt whether she honestly believes that he will never cheat on her.

Respect Your Deal Breakers

Most of us have deal breakers when it comes to dating. Deal breakers are things that you cannot tolerate under any circumstances and that undoubtedly put an end to a relationship. Maybe you absolutely don't date stoners, smokers, or habitual liars. In a perfect world where everyone is completely honest and upfront, a handsome guy would tell you on the first date that he does drugs or he lies all the time. I'm sure you won't be going out with him again. However, if you only came to find out after entering a relationship with him, it may be a harder decision to break up with him.

Once we have built an emotional connection, especially with someone that we planned to share a happy ending with, it's much harder to stick to our deal breaker policy. I'm here to tell you that your deal breakers exist for a reason. Think about the reason that they are your deal breakers in the first place. No guy is worth the justification for you to change your deal breakers or compromise on your values so that this guy can fit into your life.

If He Doesn't Like You Back, He Doesn't Deserve You

If, after you've had the "where is this going" conversation with your dream guy, and he clearly isn't interested in investing in a long-term relationship with you, it is time to take him at his word and believe him. I know it's heartbreaking to walk away when you have finally met a guy who seems to be everything you ever wanted in a lifelong partner. But, if he doesn't like you back, he isn't worth your time and attention.

You shouldn't settle for a guy that may only be seeing you once a week without showing you affection for the rest of the week, regardless of how great the night you spend with him is, or how happy he makes you feel in that moment. You shouldn't settle for that. You deserve to be happy with someone seven days a week! I'm not saying he needs to be with you every day, of course, but he needs to treat you the way you deserve to be treated.

At times, you may become discouraged on your path to finding an ideal boyfriend, but keep going and believe it will happen. Under no circumstances should you lower your standards and settle for less than what you deserve. One day, you will thank yourself for not giving in.

Better a Little Loss
Than a Long Sorrow

In all the three scenarios above, it is probably going to be excruciatingly hard to end the relationship with him. He is the guy that you've come to know well. You even thought he would be the one! The last thing you want to hear is that it's time for you to go out there and start this journey all over again. Compared to that heartache, it seems much easier to try to keep the relationship where it is, hoping one day that he is going to change.

However, better a little loss than a long sorrow. If you stick with him, you are dragging yourself into his trouble and wasting years of your life. You will become even more emotionally attached. This happened to me, too.

I was dating this guy for two months and I thought I was his girlfriend already, only to realize that he hid a secret from me. I learned that he needed to smoke marijuana every day in order to function. That was a complete deal breaker for me. I cried for days because it was so painful to leave him, and it seemed so unlikely that I would meet anyone as good as he was!

Two months after deciding to leave him, I received more bad news: My work visa was having problems and it was ultimately denied two months later. I started long-distance running or biking almost every day just to be able to function without crying or mentally collapsing. During one bike ride, I fell off my bike and injured both knees. Bad things kept happening to me. I kept wishing I hadn't broke it off with him so I wouldn't be in such sorrow, at least in the relationship department.

I didn't completely get over him until I started a serious relationship with my now husband. He helped me realize that I didn't even know someone could be this amazing while treating me the way a woman should be treated, in every possible way. Countless times I have told myself, *Thank God I didn't give in and lower my standards and settle with that pothead.* Trust me, as hard and impossible as it may feel now, you will eventually meet your Mr. Right. Remember, the fastest way to find the right guy is to delete all the wrong ones from your life as soon as possible.

Learn Something New

The more you liked him, the harder it will be to get your mind off the breakup. You may find yourself crying your day away or drinking alcohol to fall asleep, in tears. It's natural to be sad, and as easy as it can be to let your emotions go, these behaviors are neither healthy nor graceful. At the end of the day, you were smart enough to have realized that he wasn't the right one and you were strong enough to end the whole deal. Therefore, you are also resilient enough to now be able to bounce back gracefully.

The one and only way that has helped me go through those low days with positivity was to live in the moment. However, it is easier said than done. This is where learning something new comes into play. We all have something in the back of our mind that we would love to do when we have time, when we are not this busy, or even when we are retired. Now that you aren't spending time with him, and probably are not ready to see other guys yet, why don't you take advantage of this time and learn something new? When we learn something new, it makes living in the moment natural, because you are focused on something. A new hobby makes living in the moment your default position. When you concentrate on a new skill, you don't have a lot of mental room to dwell on the past.

I decided to learn ice skating when I finally recovered from my knee injury. When I was on ice, I had to keep concentrating on not falling. After spending a whole afternoon on ice, I realized I hadn't thought about him at all for the past several hours! It was a big deal because I simply wasn't able to get my mind off him for a minute, let alone for hours. I was able to ice skate elegantly and gracefully after several months and, thanks to that experience, I was able to go ice skating with my now husband for the second date. How wonderful is that! Not only will this activity help you get over that wrong guy, you will also continue having this skill as your asset that gives you joy for the rest of your life.

Learning something new is hard, but it will be easier than getting over him. One way to push and remind yourself of this new hobby or goal is to use it as your password. Come up with a password that incorporates this new activity and use an inspiring picture of your new hobby as your screensaver. Better yet, use your favorite lipstick to write it on your mirror. This way you are reminded throughout your day about a new goal you have set for yourself.

Recap

- ✓ Cheaters are always going to cheat.
- ✓ Respect your deal breakers.
- ✓ If he doesn't like you back, he doesn't deserve you.
- ✓ Better a little loss than a long sorrow.
- ✓ When you lose someone you like from your life, go learn something new.

Step 9

GET THAT DIAMOND RING

*"Engagement marks the end of a whirlwind romance
and beginning of an eternal love story."*

— RAJEEV RANJAN

*A*re you ready for him to put a ring on it? There are questions you need to ask yourself and him before you know you are ready to marry him. There are also warning signs to help you see that you are never going to be his fiancée. If you are both in agreement that marriage is on the table, how can you make your dream happen?

Before You Say Yes

You probably only want to get engaged once in your lifetime. For this reason, you need to be one hundred percent sure that you want to be his wife, and that he is going to treat you the way you deserve. Here are two sets of questions to help you decide. Ask yourself the first set of questions. If, and only if all of your answers are genuinely positive, move on to the second set of questions for him. After you have satisfactory answers from him, you know you are truly ready to say yes if he proposes.

First set of questions, ask yourself:

1.   Are you ready to be a wife?

Are you emotionally ready for the most invasive thing that will happen in your life? This person will know when you are pooping and probably hear it. He will be there when you are at the peak of your career and when your parents pass away. He will see the version of you that you have been hiding from the public, and you will discover he drinks juice right out of the carton and leaves toenail clippers in the kitchen. You need to be prepared to see the whole, natural, and true sides of both of you, not just the romantic stuff you see in the movie.

2. **Does the thought of being his wife make you feel happy or stuck?**

   When you think about spending the rest of your life with him as a wife, does it make you feel happy and excited or feel stuck in a rut? If you are ready to be his wife, you will look forward to spending every day with him forever, instead of getting scared that you are going to be stuck with him.

3. **Is he meeting the standard to be your husband?**

   There is going to be some time between getting engaged and getting married, but certain things won't change over such a short time, if ever. Does he need to stop smoking so you can happily marry him? If he doesn't want kids, but you know you would love to be a mom, are you waiting for him to change his mind? If he parties too much with his friends, do you expect him to suddenly stop once you are married? If he isn't meeting your standards to be your future husband, he won't make a great husband after you are really married. Remember, you can't change who he is.

4. **Are you OK with only having sex with him for the rest of your life?**

   Sex with him should be amazing and meet both of your needs in bed. Along with friendship, sex is another key to a long and lasting marriage. Studies have been done on the effects of sex in regard to marriage. These studies have shown that having sex leads to increased bonding between couples.[2] There is also a popular "30-Day Sex Challenge" that couples with marriage problems credit for saving their marriages. Admittedly, sex isn't the only thing that saved their marriages, but it makes all other things necessary to make a marriage work again effortless.

5. **Is he your friend?**

Friendship tends to be undervalued when it comes to marriage. When we think about marriage, we think about love. In fact, friendship is a huge part of the foundation to make a marriage work for the decades to come. You should be able to have enjoyable conversations with him and get his sense of humor. You should enjoy spending time with him. You should desire his companionship day and night. Friendship will be one of the most important factors later down the road, when romance wears off and things start to get into a routine. "All love that has not friendship for its base, is like a mansion built upon the sand." – Ella Wheeler Wilcox.

6. **Are you comfortable discussing hard topics with him?**

Even if you are best friends with your husband, it doesn't

---

2   https://journals.sagepub.com/doi/full/10.1177/0956797617691361

necessarily mean you are comfortable discussing hard topics with him. Are you two comfortable talking about money? Do you have similar financial goals or is one of you a spender and the other a saver? Have you discussed about how often you should have sex? Are you OK with the other party watching pornography? How about each other's sexual fantasy? If asking him these questions will make you uncomfortable, your relationship isn't ready for marriage.

7. Can you handle him when he is at his worst?
Good times are easy on everyone, but how about bad times? Have you seen him through a bad and hard time? Are you OK with how he responds to a hard situation? For example, if he is gentlemanly and sweet when he is in a good mood, but blames you for everything when things are not going well, should you accept it? If he appears to be calm and rooted when everything is working out the way he wants, but he gets overly anxious and emotionally abusive when things happen out of his control, are you really going to be OK with it? If he is loyal to you when life is treating him well, but feels the need to get validation from multiple other women when things are going bad, is this what you want? These are serious things to consider. Remember the red flags we already talked about.

8. Does he make compromises to make you happy?

If he cannot stand love and romance movies but those are your favorite, does he watch them with you even though he is cringing the entire time? If he doesn't like Korean food but you absolutely love it, does he have it with you from time to time? If he goes raiding with his friends every Tuesday and Wednesday night, but you say you would like to spend more time with him, does he make any adjustments? Of course, making compromises isn't a one-way street; we all need to compromise sometimes. His willingness to go through mildly unpleasant moments to make you happy is a significant aspect of a long-lasting marriage.

If all of your answers to these eight questions are "yes," move on to the second set of questions that you need to ask him:

9. "If I lose my job, will you provide for me until I get back on my feet?"

This question gives you a more detailed idea on how willing he is to provide for you. Everyone goes through tough financial times and, as your husband, he should be able to support you through yours. He may be doing a great job providing for you right now when you are bringing money to the table, but you need to have an idea of what to expect when things go south.

10. "If I get into a dispute with your family, who will you support?"

There is no standard or correct answer here, but you need to look at his reasoning and thinking process when he is put in this situation. His answer should include that he will be able to handle the conflict wisely, and that he will support you when the dispute arises. You both need to be realistic about whether your parents are overbearing or if his parents treat him like a child. Remember, you aren't just marrying him. You are marrying into a new family and both of you need to be clear about your expectations and be honest about your extended family dynamic. Problems with in-laws can be a huge part of an unhappy marriage.

Ask the next two questions if you both want to have children in the future. They will help you get a better feel for how he would act as a husband and a father.

11. Do you both have the same parenting vision or adhere to the same standards when it comes to parenting?

If you don't share a basic parenting vision on simple issues, it will cause conflict later down the road. For example, if your kid wants to eat ice cream without having any regular meals, you both need to be on the same page. If you think it's unacceptable, but he gives in, it will be inevitable that you end up blowing up at him a lot. This is unhealthy for both of your relationship and your kid's mental health. There are a lot of parenting books you can read, and everyone has their own style when it comes to dealing with their children. The key is that you both present a united front and aren't undermining each other. You need to be in agreement on how you want to raise children.

12. Do you want your kid to be raised in one religion or another?

If you are a Buddhist and your husband is agnostic, do you want to raise your kid as a Buddhist? If Christianity is important for you but you don't want to force a certain religion on your kid, is he going to be ok with it? Religion and children can be a huge issue, especially if your extended families are very religious. This needs to be something you decide beforehand.

If any of these four questions come out as a flashing red light, it is in your best interest to reconsider whether he is the right person to be your future husband.

You, Not Him, Decide
When to Get Engaged

Lots of women fall into this trap of cautiously being the best girlfriend she can possibly be while waiting for him to bring up the marriage topic. Or worse, some girls I know are too scared to even bring up the word. They call it "The M word." In fact, marriage should be an ongoing conversation that starts naturally. It's not something that you both carefully avoid talking about, but then all of a sudden, comes to his mind. While the proposal should be a surprise, you shouldn't be surprised that he is going to propose at some point. You guys should have talked about the idea already.

Here is a good way to start talking about marriage for the first time: Focus on the idea of marriage as a generic subject first and bring it up casually during your conversations. Eventually, tell him your expected timeline to get married.

1. Focus on the idea of marriage in general.
    Instead of starting a conversation about the potential marriage between you two, bring up the idea in normal conversations. When you watch a romance movie together, say something like "Aww. The idea of marriage is great! You love one and only one person for the rest

of your life." or if you are talking about travelling, try casually bringing up "I'm saving the Aegean Sea for my honeymoon." You can also ask him "How about you?"

2. Talk about the idea of you and him becoming a married couple.

When the relationship has deepened, and after having brought it up casually for several times, talk about the idea of you two getting married. For example, I remember when my husband was still my boyfriend, we were walking down the road after dinner and we saw this cute old couple. He held her hand and she leaned her head on his shoulder when they were waiting for the red light. We both saw it at the same time, we looked at each other, and kissed. I then whispered to him gently with love, "I wish we could be like that when we grow old." Another example is when we watched a movie at home that involved a married couple having conflicts, we would talk about how we would have handled the situation on the screen.

3. Bring up your expected timeline to get married.

Do this after he is comfortable with the idea of you two as a married couple and when you feel certain that he wants you for the rest of his life. If you plan on being married by a certain age, let him know that. Remember how you say it is more important than what you say.

Be confident and calm when things get a bit agitating during the talk.

Don't Let Your Friends and Family Work Against You

After you've conveyed your expected timeline on getting engaged, make sure to leave it as it is. Please refrain any urge to keep nagging him why he hasn't proposed yet. This also applies to your friends and family.

I have a friend called Sally. She was in a steady relationship with William, her boyfriend for four years. Everything seemed to be going well but they never talked about getting engaged, while Sally and her family had been secretly waiting for William to propose. Every time Sally posts a loving picture of her and William, Sally's family members would comment "Time to pop the question, William!" or "Has he proposed yet?" William never responded to any of these comments, and Sally usually responded with "Nope. I agree he needs to propose though!" One day, I heard that they broke up.

Three months later, Sally changed her Facebook status to "in a relationship" with another guy, Bob. Sally was a beautiful girl and clearly this guy seemed to be hooked from the beginning. Six months passed. Sally posted some cute pictures of them in the love capital of the world, Paris. Again, her family members flooded the comment area with comments like "OMG! Bob, I think it is a great place to propose!"

Other family members chimed in with comments like "Yes! Put a ring on it! Don't be a chicken. Sally won't bite!" Sally was responding to every one of these awkward comments, but Bob didn't even click on the "like" button. One of the family members even said, "Aren't you two married already?" I don't know whether that relative was trying to be funny, but she forced Sally to respond with "Nope, but that's the goal someday." Bob's lack of response and Sally's continual explanations did nothing but make Sally look very desperate.

When Bob casually posts a picture with Sally, Sally's cousin leaves a comment: "Hi Bob, this is Sally's cousin. I don't live in your area so I don't know when I will meet you, but Mary, Sally's mother, speaks very highly of you. I think it's time for you two to be engaged." This kind of cyber-meddling is over the top. Not only are they pressuring Sally and Bob, but these outside expectations voiced on social media are unnecessary. Sally comes across as a desperate spinster and Bob looks like a dispassionate boyfriend.

Sally's example is probably more on the extreme end, but you get the idea. Don't let your friends or family work against you. Nip any kind of interference in the bud. Your family members undoubtedly have opinions, but in the end, their opinions don't need to add pressure to your relationship or create a wedge between you and your boyfriend. Don't let them inject themselves into your business. If you can see yourself in Sally's example, you need to assert yourself and set boundaries with family members. You are in control of your future; they aren't.

Signs that You Are NEVER Going to be His Fiancée

If you are still on the fence or you and your boyfriend still have a long way to go before being able to comfortably talk about the idea of marriage, here are six signs that you probably won't be the girl that he ends up proposing to. If you see yourself or your boyfriend in this list, please do some self-reflection and decide if it's time to move on.

1. He doesn't open up to you.

   Men are naturally less willing to share their feelings compared to women. They grew up being told to be brave and strong and many men equate being vulnerable with being weak. However, when a guy sees you as his future wife, he is going to be comfortable opening up to you. He will feel safe showing you his vulnerable side without feeling the risk of appearing weak. Thus, if your guy seldom shows his emotional side in front of you, he might not see you as his future wife. For example, he will talk about news and politics with you, but shuts down and doesn't express his feelings when his grandpa passes away. If you think your guy is emotionally detached and you believe it is just his personality, trust me, that is how he is in front of you. He won't be the same in front of his future wife.

2. He isn't quite protective and providing.

Guys are naturally protective, and they have the innate urge to provide for the women they truly love. No matter whether it is holding your hand when crossing the street or letting you walk on the inner side of the sidewalk, you will feel the sense of being protected by him. If he seldom makes you feel that way and claims that you are a strong woman so you don't need his protection, it could either because he is still a little boy or he doesn't see you as the girl that he wants to protect. Same thing goes with providing. When a guy loves you and wants to spend the rest of his life with you, it is inevitable that he is going to provide for you. It doesn't matter how much money he makes, he will give you the best that he can offer, even if it means that he won't be able to afford the best things that he wants.

3. He doesn't ask your opinion before he makes major decisions.

If he is making a major decision that will impact his life and may also affect his relationship with you, he will ask for your opinion and consider your feelings seriously. Let's say you are in a relationship with him and he wants to buy a house. If he sees marrying you in the near future, he is going to get your opinion on buying a house. Even if he is just planning on renting it out after marrying you, he would still ask your opinion on where the house is and how practical it will be to be rented out.

What if he wants to apply for a top law school when his current job appointment is over? He will ask you about relocating and talking about whether a long-distance relationship is feasible. He will see himself with you after he graduates. These are things you need to discuss. When you marry someone, you should both be in agreement about major life decisions.

Financially speaking, making big decisions without consulting your partner can really hurt the relationship. It's no secret that money problems are a leading cause of divorce. If you have separate bank accounts in your marriage, is the person who makes less money paying for utilities and groceries while the other spouse has lots of extra money to buy expensive toys? Both of you need to agree on big purchases and how to budget money. If he does not involve you in financial decisions, he might be devaluing your importance in the relationship. This is a warning sign that he doesn't see you as his long term partner.

4. He doesn't take care of you.

As straightforward as this can be, some guys stay in relationships because of the convenience she brings. For instance, if he travels for work a lot and he has a dog, does he take it for granted that you will watch his dog all the time? If you are sick, and he does see you as his future wife, he will make sure you have everything you need. He will pay for your Uber eats and makes sure to bring you medicine or pick up a prescription. He will tuck you in and wrap you like a little burrito. Mr. Wrong would probably say some sweet things and still leave his dog with you!

5. You don't feel confident communicating your life goal timeline with him.

However shy and introverted you are, if you see yourself marrying this guy in the future, you need to have the courage to tell him the desired timeline of your life. For example, it shouldn't be too hard for you to tell him "I would like to get married by 35." If you are a strong and powerful woman at work, but you don't feel confident enough to bring this up to him, you need to admit that this relationship isn't going too well. You may need to do some soul searching and ask yourself why you lack this confidence in your personal relationships. Understanding yourself better will help you grow in future relationships.

In a worst-case scenario, you may adore him so much that you find yourself delaying your life goal timeline just to stay with him. You may want to get married by 35, but you don't see that happening with him, so you tell yourself that age isn't really that big of a deal. This is an ultimate sign that he will never be your future husband. Waiting or changing your timeline won't give him enough time to be ready to marry you. It will only waste the prime years of your precious life.

6. You don't feel brave enough to confront him when you suspect him of having an affair.

    This one can be a bit extreme, but unfortunately it does happen. When your boyfriend is acting a little strange, he brings his phone wherever he goes, seems more emotionally distant from you than normal, or is unreachable during prolonged hours, you should feel something is off. You have suspicions but you are scared to look for signs or confront him, because you don't want to face the fact that he might be having an affair. In this case, neither one of you is ready for marriage. You are definitely not the one he has in mind to walk down the aisle with, if he ever intends to marry at all. If you do find out he's cheating, remember what I said earlier. Once a cheater, always a cheater.

How to Make Your Dream Proposal Happen

Every girl deserves to be proposed by her dream guy in the exact way she desires. Believe it or not, it's partly your job to make it happen. Proposing is one of the most frightening things for a guy to do. They need to make sure they plan it the way you like, keep everything a secret while making it as perfect as it can possibly be, and yet they still need to stay calm and put together so they don't look like a complete idiot in front of you. It is a lot of pressure! In order to make your dream proposal happen, there are things you can do to make the act of proposing easier.

I don't recommend taking the burden off him completely by saying it's OK if he doesn't do a real proposal. Here is the rule: You need to tell him what you want the proposal to be like, but let him put it together and surprise you. Tell him if you want the proposal to be private or if you want it to be done in public. If you want your friends and family to be there in a certain way, you need to make sure he knows.

If you think proposal photos are as important as wedding pictures, it is absolutely necessary to convey this message too. If you normally don't get manicures, but you want your hands to look perfect in your proposal pictures, you must point that out to him ahead of time. The worst thing you want is to have ragged nails in your engagement pictures and blame him after everything is over. However, it is his job to figure out how to get you in that nail salon or how to sneak in a photographer to the proposal.

The other big part of the proposal is the engagement ring. It doesn't matter if you are a diamond girl or an unconventional sapphire girl. Whether you don't care about the brand of the ring or you are a die-hard Tiffany girl, it is your job to let him know that. A good idea is to casually point out "Aww, I want my engagement ring to be like that," when you see an engagement ring on a commercial or simply be straightforward and send him a picture of the ring you want.

If you are not sure what ring you like, ask him to go ring shopping with you so you can try them on. When it comes to your ring size, it is a good idea to tell your mom or your best friend, or whomever he will most likely reach out to for help! After you've done your job, it is his job to do the research and find the best ring within his budget.

Recap

- Eight questions to ask yourself, along with four questions to ask him before you agree on marrying him.

- Marriage is a continuing conversation rather than a sudden idea. You, not him, decide when to get engaged.

- Continue to strive to be a better version of yourself and appear to be the highest value in his eyes.

- Don't let your friends or family work against you.

- Six signs that you probably won't be the woman that he ends up proposing to.

- How to make your dream proposal happen.

BE THE GODDESS BRIDE, NOT THE ETERNAL FIANCÉE

" You look like the rest of my life."

—BEAU TAPLIN

According to Weddingwire, the average couple is engaged for 13 months. If you are fine with staying engaged forever, this chapter isn't for you. However, if you would like to walk down the aisle with him in the near future, this chapter will tell you the two key aspects to make it happen. I will also share with you how to have a stress-free wedding.

Don't Act Like His Wife Already

When it comes to steak or wine, the more aged the better. But a fiancée is different. You want to get married, not to be his fiancée for the decades to come. The principle is not to act like his wife when he is just your fiancé.

Compared to being a girlfriend, the difference between being a wife and a fiancée is much smaller, but there is still a fine line between the two. When you were just dating, you probably spent 10-20 percent of your spare time together, and that increased to 30–50 percent when he became your boyfriend. As fiancée, it is desirable to spend 60–70 percent of the time together, but not 90 percent or more. Make time for yourself, keep leveling up, and keep being the hottest You.

Also, keep off all the future husband's benefits until after you both have walked down the aisle and said "I do." Your husband gets to live with you, but your fiancé doesn't. Your husband gets to have sex with you without a condom if you are on birth control, but your fiancé doesn't. In order to not stay stuck in the engaged zone, you need to give him something to look forward to that's exclusively available to your husband.

Set the Wedding Date!

Another factor to ensure you get married in the foreseeable future is to set the wedding date. Planning a wedding is exciting, but it also requires a lot of energy and money. A lot of couples eventually lose the momentum of planning and having a wedding after staying engaged for too long when the joy of engagement dies off and the idea of a wedding is more overwhelming than exciting.

Ideally, you and your fiancé should discuss the wedding date as soon as possible after you get engaged. You probably won't be able to decide on a date right away, as it requires a lot of consideration, but you need to have the conversation with him and get the process going ASAP. Doing so within the period of excitement and joy of your engagement will make the process a lot easier. Also, planning a wedding can be incredibly stressful, so it's best to set the date and plan a bit on the early side. This gives you less to worry about when the big day arrives.

Until the date that you walk down the aisle, continue to improve yourself and be the hottest bride! Use your time as a fiancée to solidify how the details of the marriage will work. Many couples go to pre-marital counselling. Whether you do that or not, you need to have heart-to-heart conversations about important details of your marriage. For instance, you may want to join bank accounts, phone plans, or insurance to save money. Do you agree on a budget? Will there be debt to pay off? It's also a good time to start making arrangements on where you two are going to live after getting married. You may move in with him, he may be the one to move in with you depending when leases end, or you may want to purchase your house together.

Have a Stress-Free Wedding Day

The wedding day should be one of the most special days in a woman's life. You get to be dressed in the most gorgeous wedding dress, walking toward the love of your life, in front of your friends and family. However, the wedding day can also end up being one of the most stressful days for some women.

This is understandable. There are a million things that could go wrong. Your mind will be worrying about every single detail! *Hopefully, the venue turns out to be lovely with all the centerpieces and guests seated. The table linens better come out perfectly matching with the color of bridesmaid dresses. What if guests keep showing up late? Our first dance has to be perfect. Oh my God, if it rains then my wedding day is going to be ruined!*

These are just a couple of things that brides tend to worry about before and during their big day. You may be especially stressed if you are your own wedding planner. It is common to have the urge of having a perfect wedding, but if you spend so much energy worrying that you end up missing genuine moments in that priceless day, it is really worth it?

The key to having a stress-free wedding day is to be mindful. Being mindful means to be aware of the current moment. Have all of your senses and attention in that moment; not past regrets, not future worries. When you get your makeup done with your bridesmaids, enjoy their companionship instead of worrying whether all the makeup will be done on time. When you walk down the aisle, enjoy being wrapped in all the love, rather than being anxious whether you are walking down the aisle in perfect sync with the music. When you dance the night away with your new husband, immerse yourself in the passion and love as opposed to looking around all the time making sure all of your guests are happy. The wedding is about you and the love of your life! It slips by fast, so grasp every second of it by being mindful and living at the moment.

If you know someone in your family who is a perfectionist and has a tendency to get frustrated when things don't go as planned, make sure to have a talk with him or her before the wedding. I was blessed to have my amazing future mother-in-law as my wedding planner. She was the best wedding planner one could possibly have, but I wanted to make sure she wouldn't react negatively if the wedding didn't flow as planned. I told her that if anything goes wrong during the wedding, it is OK. I preferred it to be a happy and relaxing wedding rather than a perfect and stressful one.

The night before my wedding, I was so excited that I barely slept. My heart was constantly beating so fast that I could feel it coming out of my chest! When the wedding day arrived, I tried my best to live in the moment and enjoy all of the love and support from my bridesmaids and my family. I even took breaks during the day to write mini journals in my phone about what was happening and how I was feeling at the moment. However, my excitement or nervousness started getting a bit out of control when we all arrived at the venue, and I was about ready to walk down the aisle.

I got so emotional and nervous that I completely forgot to enjoy every second of the special night. However, it all changed after one of my bridesmaids, Elizabeth, said something to the bridal group. She suggested all of us take a deep breath, looking around at what was happening around us, fully living in the moment, and enjoying it one hundred percent. That was the moment that changed everything. That moment, along with what happened after that, is still what I remember most clearly from the wedding day.

Finding the love of your life and being able to see him standing in front of you as you walk down the aisle is one of the hardest things to do. I am so proud that you are taking action toward it, and I know you will make it happen! Let me know your success stories and invite me to your wedding! You can reach me at swipetothealtar@gmail.com.

Recap

- ✅ Don't act like his wife already.
- ✅ Set the wedding date.
- ✅ Have a stress-free wedding day.

Conclusion

$\mathcal{N}$ow that you've finished reading the entire book, you are fully aware of how to find your true love online. This is more than a book. It is a real and practical way of finding love.

It is now up to you to take action, if you haven't started already. If you don't use these steps and techniques in your real life, they won't help your love life at all. I know there will be some people that will read it but go back to their old single life after putting the book back on the shelf.

In fact, a lot of people do tons of research and read all the books on the topic without taking any action. They may be able to tell you exactly what each book said and what each dating coach suggested, but unfortunately, they will never find their true love online if they don't make a move. I don't want this to happen to you. Now that you have finished reading the last chapter, your countdown to finding true love online has officially begun. Think about why you wanted to read this book in the first place, take action, and *Swipe to the Altar* now.

Your friend and coach,

Mrs. Q. Warnock.

Acknowledgements

J want to first honor my husband, my best friend, and the love of my life, Chris. Thank you for being you and for creating the great love I always hoped would happen. Thank you for encouraging me throughout the process of writing this book. I am honored to be your wife and your life partner. I love you. I would like to honor my parents, Yaming Li and Chunyan Zhang. Thank you for letting me follow my heart and love.

I also want to honor my coach, Scott Allan. Thank you for guiding me every step of the journey publishing my first book. I want to honor my editor, Jennifer Bradshaw. Thank you for teaming up with me and helping give this book its heart. I want to thank Matthew Hussey, the life and dating coach I've been following since 2013 when my journey looking for true love began. Thank you for the seminars, videos, and the book, *How to Talk to Guys*, that have helped me tremendously and made me become who I am today.

I would like to give my last special thanks to two of my friends. He Huang, thank you for talking me into trying on-line dating in 2014 and staying by my side during the ups and downs over the years. Meghann Geiger, thank you for encouraging me to join Tinder in 2016. Never in my wildest dreams would I imagine marrying such an amazing husband without you girls and online dating. Thank you for making that happen.

About the Author

Mrs. Q. Warnock, the former Miss Qianlei Li, started her online dating journey in 2014 and found the love of her life at the end of 2016. She has gone on 42 first dates and has got her heart broken multiple times before realizing the right way to go about online dating. She now lives happily with her husband in Northern Virginia.

Thank You

Thank you so much for sticking with me to the end. It would mean a lot to me if you go to Amazon.com and leave an honest review about this book. It's completely free to do so, and you will help other women like you tremendously. You make me proud! Thank you!

CPSIA information can be obtained
at www.ICGtesting.com
Printed in the USA
LVHW082144140820
663150LV00007B/413